THE SOPRANOS℠

FAMILY COOKBOOK

AS COMPILED BY ARTIE BUCCO

THE Sopranos SM

FAMILY COOKBOOK

AS COMPILED BY ARTIE BUCCO

by Allen Rucker

Recipes by Michele Scicolone

Series created by David Chase

HBO®

IT'S NOT TV. IT'S HBO.™

BRADGREY
TELEVISION

WARNER BOOKS

NEW YORK   BOSTON

Warner Books

Time Warner Book Group
1271 Avenue of the Americas, New York, NY 10020
Visit our Web site at www.twbookmark.com.

Printed in the United Kingdom
by Butler & Tanner Ltd, Frome and London
First Printing: September 2002
20 19 18 17 16 15 14 13

ISBN: 0-446-53057-3
LCCN: 2002106752

Book Design by Mada Design, Inc./NYC

To all of our mothers,
no matter what they cook.

Acknowledgments

Many, many thanks to: David Chase, Ilene Landress, Russell Schwartz, Sandra Bark, Michele Scicolone, Ellen Silverman, Carolyn Strauss, Miranda Heller, Richard Oren, Martin Felli, John Ventimiglia, Federico Castelluccio and cast and crew, Sandra Vannucchi, Nona Jones, Victoria Frazier, Chris Newman, the gracious staff of the New Jersey Information Center, and the incomparable assistance of Bree Conover and Felicia Lipchik. Also, I'd like to thank Ann-Marie, Blaine, and Max for all their love and support.

—Allen Rucker

Thank you to Ilene Landress for never getting depressed with all the meetings it took to produce this book. We already thanked our mothers, so thank you to my grandmother, Theresa Melfi, one of the world's great cooks and also my father, Henry Chase who was a really good cook, pie maker, and, perhaps more important, convinced me to eat mussels and clams. To most of my relatives—they are good at the stove, my wife, Denise, and her mother, Simone Kelly, where I first experienced French food, and also to my daughter, Michele with whom we've had a lot of happy, delicious lunches and dinners.

—David Chase

Contents

ARTIE BUCCO

Introduction
by Artie Bucco

NUOVO VESUVIO RISTORANTE, ESSEX COUNTY, NEW JERSEY

Ciao! Benvenuti alla mia cucina! *To all of you, I say, "Hello, and welcome to my kitchen!" Actually, I'm inviting you into many kitchens, many* Italian-American *kitchens, and, along the way, into many Italian-American lives. If you are one of us, either by birth or in spirit, you know that food is not just fuel for the Italian body. Food is* la gioia di vivere, *zest for life. Food is family, tradition, birth, confirmation, marriage, sickness, death—life itself. A* paisan *without food is like Cecilia Bartoli without a song. Why get up in the morning?*

This Italian-American cookbook does not come from some loudmouth TV chef trying to get rich off of "Risotto al Funghi" or a brainy "student" of Italian cooking who learned it all in a weekend at a high-priced gastronomium in California. This book of meals comes from real life, la vita reale. *The recipes are real, the people who cook them do so in real kitchens, for real families, and many get real fat! The* cuochi, *or chefs, are my friends, or in some cases, me, and they are all non-pros, except, of course, me. We live in northern New Jersey, the true "garden" of the Garden State, and although we come from many walkways of life and have our own private victories, defeats, and tie games, we share a common* passione *for the food*

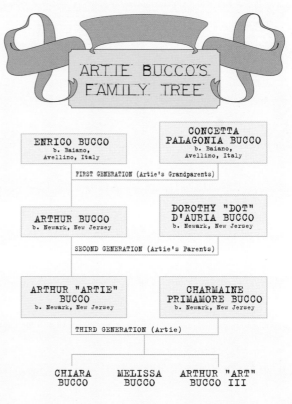

ARTIE BUCCO'S FAMILY TREE

| ENRICO BUCCO
b. Baiano, Avellino, Italy | CONCETTA PALAGONIA BUCCO
b. Baiano, Avellino, Italy |

FIRST GENERATION (Artie's Grandparents)

| ARTHUR BUCCO
b. Newark, New Jersey | DOROTHY "DOT" D'AURIA BUCCO
b. Newark, New Jersey |

SECOND GENERATION (Artie's Parents)

| ARTHUR "ARTIE" BUCCO
b. Newark, New Jersey | CHARMAINE PRIMAMORE BUCCO
b. Newark, New Jersey |

THIRD GENERATION (Artie)

| CHIARA BUCCO | MELISSA BUCCO | ARTHUR "ART" BUCCO III |

ZUPPE:
MINESTRONE

SPAGHETTI
WITH MEATBALLS

VEAL PARMIGIANO

RAVIOLI

LASAGNE

CHICKEN CACCIATORE

STEAK PIZZAIOLA

VINO / CAFFÈ / WATER

our forefathers and mothers brought with them from "the old country." This cookbook is our humble attempt to pass this culinary blessing on to you, the reader.

Before we start to boil the water and sauté the garlic, a few words about myself. I am a third-generation Italian-American chef and restaurateur. My grandparents, Enrico and Concetta Bucco, came from the province of Avellino in Southern Italy in 1913, leaving behind a legacy of poverty and exploitation. But they had each other and a love that could move mountains. With uncommon courage, they followed their dream and opened their first hole-in-the-wall restaurant, Bucco's Vesuvio— named after the volcano of their youth—in the heavily Italian First Ward of Newark, New Jersey, in 1926. Their rice balls were soon known as far away as Hackensack.

My father, Arthur, and my dear mother, Dot, followed their dream by following

Dear Mama:
I miss you very much. It is cold here and the heat in our building went out and we must wear heavy coats & gloves to bed. Please send recipe for rice balls. Many ask for them and I want to make them right. Am now working as ditch digger, but pay is low, the *padrone* is a bastard, and I often get sick. Concetta says we should start our own restaurant. What a dreamer! Wish you were here. Give my love to Papa. Your loving son, Enrico

Cara Mamma':
    Tu me manc'verament' assaiJe. Ca' fa fridd' e o' riscaldament dà casa nostra nun funziona percio' quanno ce iamm a cucca' ce avimma mettere guant e cappott' pe' ce scarfa. Pe' piacer' manname a' ricetta re' ppall'e' riso.
    Nu sacc' e' ggente e' vva' truanno e io e' voglio fa' comme si deve. Mo' io sto' faticanno comme scavatore de muort, pero' e' sord so' 'ppochi e o' titolare e' nu' bbastard e io caro spiss'malat. Concetta continua a dicere ca' nuJie ce avessem' arapi' nu' ristorante do' nuosto! Ei'che sunnatrice. Vulese tanto ca' tu stisse cca' cu'nuJie.
    Abbracciame a' Papa'.
        O' figlio vuost' devoto, Enrico.

ROMEO & SONS,LTD. CHROMOLITHOGRAPHY, SUTTON PLACE, NEW YORK, 04

POST CARD

Mrs. Sophia Concetta Bucco
Baiano Post Office
Baiano, Avellino
        ITALY

This side for the Address only.

the migration of second-generation Italians to the green grass of the suburbs. They opened the second Bucco's Vesuvio, also in Newark but near Bloomfield, New Jersey, in the early 1950s. When they retired to Brick Township, NJ, the keys to the front door were handed to me, fresh out of cooking school in London. That day I became the keeper of the Bucco flame. But then in 1999, tragedy struck in the form of a mysterious three-alarm fire and my dream was suddenly and cruelly asphyxiated. Yet how, I wondered, could I let that flame die? Soon my wife, Charmaine, and I opened the third Vesuvio, called Nuovo Vesuvio, also in the Essex County area. Please come by and sample our best. Reservations are recommended.

It was a labor of love for me to gather these cherished recipes in one book. Over half of the entries come from my dear friends, the multigenerational Soprano family, which includes my oldest friend, Tony Soprano, a waste management consultant in the area. He, above anyone I know, is a lover of la tavola. Also, his poker club relationship with a local literary agent allowed me to get this book off the ground with much less "shoe leather" and also at a better agency percentage than would be typical for a first-time writer.

Thus, our mutual decision to call this The Sopranos Family Cookbook. *When you come right down to it, it really should be called* The Northern New Jersey/ Friends of Artie Bucco/ Neapolitan-Avellinese Italian-American Cookbook, *but a food writer friend laughed me out of the room on that one. Tony and I liked the name Soprano—it was both catchy and well known in the area.*

Did you notice the words "Neapolitan" and "Avellinese" I slipped in there? Neapolitan means Naples, of which Avellino is an adjoining province and the revered

— 4 —

native soil of Sopranos as well as Buccos. With few exceptions, the collective authors of this cookbook hail from this general region of Southern Italy, or Campania— Napoli, Avellino, Caserta, Salerno—and so does the food they so love. Not to mince words: when the world thinks "Italian food," they're really thinking "Neapolitan food," although most people wouldn't know Naples from North Dakota. Look down at your plate—where do you think that meal came from? Spaghetti with tomato sauce? Naples. *Broccoli rabe with garlic?* Naples. *America's favorite fun food, pizza?* Napoli *again. And, as you're about to experience, there is a veritable fiesta of other Neapolitan/Avellinese dishes that you will soon be laying on the Sunday dinner table for all to ogle and awe.*

    *So, with great pride and great humility, and with the firm conviction that to know a people is to know their food, and vice versa, we offer you a healthy portion of our timeless Italian birthright—*The Sopranos Family Cookbook. ✿

NAPLES MARKET

CHAPTER ONE

Cooking the Neapolitan Way

BY NATALIE DEL GRECO, LIBRARIAN, NEWARK PUBLIC LIBRARY

*D*espite the fact that I'm the son of cooks, majored in regional Italian in cooking school, and have been to Naples twice, I don't consider myself an expert on the history of Neapolitan cooking. So I made a few calls and found one—a Newarker steeped in the culinary lore of our forefathers, a self-described "bookworm," Ms. Natalie del Greco. ✿

The authors of this exciting new cookbook have asked me to write a few words about the origins and evolution of Neapolitan cooking, which I'm honored to do. With the explosion of interest in Italian cuisine among the baby boom generation, the question of "roots" becomes all the more urgent. Although my own forefathers, like many in the Newark area, are from the province of Avellino, adjacent to Naples, I will generalize my comments to include the whole greater Neapolitan area. The important distinction is that this food did not originate in Tuscany, Rome, or Sicily. Enough said.

Neapolitan food, like the Neapolitan people, is essentially hearty and straightforward—what Middle Americans would call "stick to the ribs" food—though centuries of outside influences have also given this cuisine variety and sophistication. The area

Naples for the Asking!

READY FOR THE ADVENTURE OF A LIFETIME?
IT IS WAITING FOR YOU IN NAPOLI—NAPLES—THE GATEWAY TO
THE GRANDEUR, MYSTERY, AND JOY OF SOUTHERN ITALY.

The land of Caruso, Loren, and De Sica. Deck in the enchanting Bay of Naples on the West Coast of Italy. Eat the glorious native cuisine—Pizza Margherita, Linguine with Clams! Visit the famed Duomo of Naples or the Castel Nuovo, built in 1279! Travel to one of the wonders of the world— Mount Vesuvius, Pompeii, or Herculaneum—or the succulent vineyards of Avellino! And—best of all—fall in love with the Neapolitan people. Warm, friendly, always singing and laughing, they'll enchant you with their city, their food, their wine, and La Dolce Vita!

The ocean, the mountains, the fruit of the vine, the celestial strains of "Volare"—it's all yours on holiday in Naples. What are you waiting for? You dream of Italy. Well, Naples is calling—are you listening?

around Naples, with the sea on one side and rich mountain farmland on the other, is a veritable cornucopia of raw ingredients. Broccoli, olives, and other vegetables grow like weeds. Neapolitans were once called *mangiafoglie,* or leaf eaters, by Northern Italians because their diet was so rich in vegetables.

Then, with the influence of foreign invaders like the French and the Spanish, and the introduction of a few new ingredients, the unique cuisine of Naples began to emerge. First pasta, or in the parlance of the times, *maccerone* (macaroni), moved to the center of the table. It was easy to store for months on end and it went with almost anything.

Meanwhile, at some point, a resourceful Neapolitan came up with the idea of spreading a juicy red vegetable from the New World—the tomato—over flat bread, add a little cheese, and call it pizza. Pizza, like much of this cuisine, started out as peasant food but soon became high-class. As the story goes, one day Queen Margherita, wife of the reigning foreign overlord in the 1880s, decided to try a little of this so-called pizza. A smart *pizzaiolo* made a delicate concoction (i.e., no garlic or anchovies) with only tomatoes, mozzarella, and basil, the three colors of the Italian flag. The queen apparently loved it, the dish was dubbed Pizza Margherita, and you can now get it in Dubai and Tibet.

"Americans are like Germans!"
Q&A WITH FURIO GIUNTA

FURIO (F): *What do you want, Artie?*

ARTIE (A): *How do you like America?*

F: *I like it a lot.*

A: *How do you like the food in America?*

F: *Not so good.*

A: *How so?*

F: *First, you use too much sauce on your spaghetti. Very bad. Too soupy. Can't taste the pasta, the semolina.*

A: *I'm making a note.*

F: *Then you do something really stupid. You drink cappuccino after dinner!*

A: *Yes, that's very big here.*

F: *Well, it's stupid. Back home, cappuccino is in the morning, before 11 A.M. After dinner, it's like a, how do you say, milkshake. Americans are like Germans!*

A: *Ouch.*

F: *And, finally, never serve pasta and meat on the same plate. Very German. First the pasta, then the meat. That's the right way.*

A: *That's a lot of plates.*

F: *Make somebody to wash them. Kids here are spoil.*

A: *You must like something over here.*

F: *Yeah, my own* moozarell'*...you can't screw that up.*

A: *That's it?*

F: *No, I really like pigs in their bed. The cocktail franks. You buy frozen and heat them up.*

A: *Pigs in a blanket? You're kidding.*

F: *The dough should be soft, nice.*

A: *But you can get that* merda *anywhere.*

F: *I wish.*

Of course, the sauce of the tomato went very well with spaghetti too. The thing about pasta and tomato sauce—or any sauce—is that you can eat it constantly in an endless assortment of tastes and textures, as many young gourmands have discovered. Some experts say that it was the great Naples-born opera singer, Enrico Caruso—the Pavarotti of his day—who helped spread the cause of pasta. Being an opera singer, he had a big appetite and apparently demanded a bowl of spaghetti daily, no matter where he performed.

No doubt Caruso also craved a little pizza after a hard night of Puccini, and given the massive immigration of Neapolitans to America from 1870 onward, there was probably a pizza shop around the corner. This great influx of immigrants, mostly poor, mostly unskilled, brought the whole rich palette of Neapolitan ingredients with them—anchovies, basil, olive oil, garlic, and onions (though not in the same dish), their cheeses, and all of their preserved pork products, like salami, prosciutto, and capicola.

They even brought the idea of *take-out* pizza. Long before home pizza delivery was the American norm, street vendors in Naples would walk around with metal boxes on their heads and sell you a hot pizza right outside your kitchen window. And you can still buy it on the street there today.

For many new Italian-Americans, food became a means of economic survival. Artie Bucco's family story is a case in point. The family-run Italian restaurant quickly went from a neighborhood respite to a national cliché—the red-checked tablecloth, the straw-covered Chianti bottle, and spaghetti "with-a da meatballs" served by a guy with a handlebar mustache. Soon American capitalism was marketing spaghetti and meatballs in a can. That's what happens when you bring one of the world's great culinary treasures to this country. Americans both embrace it and debase it.

But now the clock seems to be turning back, and people everywhere are hungering for Italian food that is closer to the real thing, imbued with the ingredients and the care that "authentic" Italian food has always been given. You might say that the message of Neapolitan cooking is like the message of the people themselves: relax, sit down, serve yourself a little pasta, and *taste* life. We should all thank them for this great pleasure.

Marinara Sauce

Tomato Sauce

—〰—

Makes about 3 cups

2 large garlic cloves, lightly smashed

1/4 cup olive oil

2 pounds very ripe plum tomatoes, peeled, seeded, and chopped,
   or one 28-ounce can Italian peeled tomatoes, drained and chopped

Salt

8 to 10 fresh basil leaves, torn into pieces

──────── ✿ ✿ ✿ ────────

In a large skillet, cook the garlic in the olive oil over medium heat, pressing it occasionally with the back of a spoon, until golden, about 4 minutes.

Add the tomatoes and salt to taste. Bring to a simmer and cook, stirring often, until the sauce is thick, 15 to 20 minutes, depending on the tomatoes. Stir in the basil leaves.

Serve over hot cooked spaghetti or other pasta.

Sunday Gravy

—◊—

Makes about 8 cups

For the Sauce
2 tablespoons olive oil
1 pound meaty pork neck bones or spareribs
1 pound veal stew meat or 2 veal shoulder chops
1 pound Italian-style plain or fennel pork sausages
4 garlic cloves
1/4 cup tomato paste
Three 28- to 35-ounce cans Italian peeled tomatoes
2 cups water
Salt and freshly ground pepper
6 fresh basil leaves, torn into small pieces

For the Meatballs
1 pound ground beef or a combination of beef and pork
1/2 cup plain bread crumbs, preferably homemade
2 large eggs
1 teaspoon very finely minced garlic
1/2 cup freshly grated Pecorino Romano or Parmigiano-Reggiano
2 tablespoons finely chopped fresh flat-leaf parsley
1 teaspoon salt
Freshly ground pepper
2 tablespoons olive oil

To Serve
1 pound shells or rigatoni, cooked and still hot
Freshly grated Pecorino Romano or Parmigiano-Reggiano

—————— ✿ ✿ ✿ ——————

To make the sauce, heat the oil in a large heavy pot over medium heat. Pat the pork dry and put the pieces in the pot. Cook, turning occasionally, for about 15 minutes, or until nicely browned on all sides. Transfer the pork to a plate. Brown the veal in the same way and add it to the plate.

Place the sausages in the pot and brown on all sides. Set the sausages aside with the pork.

Drain off most of the fat from the pot. Add the garlic and cook for about two minutes or until golden. Remove and discard the garlic. Stir in the tomato paste and cook for 1 minute.

With a food mill, puree the tomatoes, with their juice, into the pot. Or, for a chunkier sauce, just chop up the tomatoes and add them. Add the water and salt and pepper to taste. Add the pork, veal, and sausages and basil and bring the sauce to a simmer. Partially cover the pot and cook over low heat, stirring occasionally, for 2 hours. If the sauce becomes too thick, add a little more water.

Meanwhile, make the meatballs:

Combine all the ingredients except the oil in a large bowl. Mix together thoroughly. Rinse your hands with cool water and lightly shape the mixture into 2-inch balls. (Note: If you are making meatballs for lasagne or baked ziti, shape the meat into tiny balls the size of a small grape.)

Heat the oil in a large heavy skillet. Add the meatballs and brown them well on all sides. (They will finish cooking later.) Transfer the meatballs to a plate.

After two hours, add the meatballs and cook for 30 minutes or until the sauce is thick and the meats very tender.

To serve, remove the meats from the sauce and set aside. Toss the cooked pasta with the sauce. Sprinkle with cheese. Serve the meats as a second course, or reserve them for another day.

Lasagne

—m—

Serves 8 to 10
Sunday Gravy (page 14) made with tiny meatballs
10 to 12 strips (10 x 4 inches each) fresh egg pasta
Salt
2 pounds whole-milk ricotta
1 pound fresh mozzarella, thinly sliced
1 1/4 cups freshly grated Parmigiano-Reggiano or Pecorino Romano,
    or a combination

———————— ✿ ✿ ✿ ————————

Remove the meats, including the meatballs, from the gravy and set aside the pork and veal. Cut the sausages into thin slices and put them with the meatballs.

Lay out some lint-free kitchen towels on a flat surface. Have a large bowl of cold water ready.

Bring at least 4 quarts of water to a boil in a large pot. Add salt to taste. Add a few pieces of the lasagne and cook until al dente, tender yet firm to the bite. Scoop the pasta out of the water and place in the cold water. When cool, lay the pasta sheets out flat on the towels. (The towels can be stacked one on top of the other.) Continue cooking and cooling the remaining lasagne in the same way.

Preheat the oven to 350°F.

Spread a thin layer of the sauce in a 13 x 9-inch baking pan. Set aside the best-looking pasta strips for the top layer. Make a layer of pasta, overlapping the pieces slightly. Spread about one-quarter of the ricotta on top of the pasta, then scatter on about one-quarter of the tiny meatballs and sliced sausages and one-quarter of the mozzarella. Spoon on about 1 cup more of the sauce and sprinkle with 1/4 cup of the grated cheese.

Repeat the layers three more times. Make a final layer of pasta, sauce, and grated cheese. (If you are making the lasagne ahead of time, cover tightly with plastic wrap and refrigerate until ready to bake, or as long as overnight.)

Bake the lasagne for 1 hour and 10 to 30 minutes, until the top is browned and the sauce is bubbling around the edges. If it starts to get too brown on top before it is heated through, cover the pan loosely with aluminum foil.

Remove the lasagne from the oven and let set for 15 minutes. Cut the lasagne into squares and serve.

Bistecca Pizzaiola

Steak Pizzaiol' ⎯⚏⎯ *Steak Pizzamaker's Style*

Serves 4

2 tablespoons olive oil
4 small tender steaks
2 large garlic cloves, finely chopped
Salt and freshly ground pepper
One 28-ounce can Italian peeled tomatoes, drained and chopped
1 teaspoon dried oregano
Pinch of crushed red pepper

⎯⎯⎯ ✿ ✿ ✿ ⎯⎯⎯

In a large skillet, heat the oil over medium heat. Pat the steaks dry. Add to the pan and cook, turning once, until browned on both sides. Sprinkle with salt and pepper. Transfer the meat to a platter.

Scatter the garlic into the pan and cook for 1 minute. Add the tomatoes, oregano, red pepper, and salt to taste. Bring the sauce to a simmer. Cook for 20 minutes, or until the sauce is thickened.

Return the steaks to the sauce. Cook briefly, turning the steaks once or twice, until they are warmed and cooked to taste. Serve hot.

Linguine alle Vongole

Linguine with White Clam Sauce

—◊◊◊—

Serves 6

3 pounds littleneck, Manila, or other small hard-shell clams
1/4 cup water
6 garlic cloves, lightly crushed
2 tablespoons chopped fresh flat-leaf parsley
1 small dried peperoncino, crumbled, or a pinch of crushed red pepper
1/2 cup extra virgin olive oil
1 pound linguine
Salt

——————— ✿ ✿ ✿ ———————

With a stiff brush, scrub the clams well under running water. Discard any clams that have broken shells or that don't close up tightly when handled.

Place the clams in a large pot with the water. Cover the pot and turn the heat to medium-high. Cook just until the clams begin to open—you will hear a popping sound. Transfer the opened clams to a bowl and continue cooking the remaining clams. Discard any that refuse to open. Set the pot aside.

Working over a small bowl to catch the juices, scrape the clams from the shells, placing them in another bowl. Pour all of the liquid from the pot into the bowl with the juices. If the clams are sandy, rinse them one at a time in the clam juices. Pass the liquid through a sieve lined with cheesecloth or a paper coffee filter.

In a 12-inch skillet, cook the garlic, parsley, and peperoncino in the oil over medium heat until the garlic is golden. Add about two-thirds of the clam juices and cook until the liquid is reduced by half. Remove and discard the garlic. Stir in the remaining juices and the clams and cook 1 minute more.

Meanwhile, bring at least 4 quarts of water to a boil in a large pot. Add the linguine and salt to taste. Cook, stirring frequently, until the linguine is al dente, tender yet still firm to the bite. Drain the pasta.

Toss the pasta with the sauce over high heat for 1 minute. Serve immediately.

Polipetti in Salsa di Pomodoro

Baby Octopus in Tomato Sauce

—m—

Serves 6

2 pounds baby octopus
2 cups peeled, seeded, and chopped fresh tomatoes or chopped canned
   Italian peeled tomatoes
1/4 cup olive oil
1/4 cup chopped fresh flat-leaf parsley
2 large garlic cloves, finely chopped
Pinch of crushed red pepper
Salt
6 to 12 friselle (black pepper biscuits) or slices toasted Italian bread

——————— ☘ ☘ ☘ ———————

Rinse the octopus and drain well. Remove the hard round beak at the base of the tentacles of each octopus.

In a large heavy saucepan, combine the octopus, tomatoes, oil, 3 tablespoons of the parsley, the garlic, red pepper, and salt to taste. Bring sauce to a simmer. Cover the pot and cook over very low heat, stirring occasionally, for 45 minutes.

Uncover the pan and cook for 15 minutes more, or until the octopus is tender when pierced with a knife and the sauce is thick.

Sprinkle the friselle with water to soften them slightly. Divide the friselle, or slices of toast, among six plates. Top with the octopus and sauce. Sprinkle with the remaining 1 tablespoon parsley and serve.

Braciole

Stuffed Beef Rolls in Tomato Sauce

—ɯ—

Serves 4

4 thin slices boneless beef round (about 1 pound)
1 garlic clove, finely chopped
2 tablespoons freshly grated Pecorino Romano
2 tablespoons chopped fresh flat-leaf parsley
Salt and freshly ground pepper
4 thin slices prosciutto
2 tablespoons olive oil
2 garlic cloves, lightly crushed
1 cup dry red wine
4 cups tomato puree, or canned Italian tomatoes passed through a food mill
4 fresh basil leaves, torn into small pieces
1 pound ziti or penne, cooked and still hot

———— ✿ ✿ ✿ ————

Place the beef between two pieces of plastic wrap and pound gently with a meat pounder or rubber mallet to a 1/4- to 1/8-inch thickness.

Sprinkle the beef with the garlic, cheese, parsley, and salt and pepper. Cover with the prosciutto slices. Roll up each piece like a sausage and tie it with kitchen string.

Heat the oil in a large pot. Add the braciole and garlic. Cook, turning the meat occasionally, until it is browned on all sides and the garlic is golden. Add the wine and simmer for 2 minutes. Remove and discard the garlic.

Stir in the tomato puree and basil.

Cover and cook over low heat, turning the meat occasionally, until it is tender when pierced with a fork, about 2 hours. Add a little water if the sauce becomes too thick.

Serve the sauce over the hot cooked ziti as a first course, followed by the braciole.

Struffoli

Honey Balls

Serves 12

About 1 1/2 cups all-purpose flour
1/4 teaspoon salt
3 large eggs
Vegetable oil for deep-frying
1 1/2 cups honey
Chopped candied orange peel, red and green candied cherries, multicolored
    candy sprinkles, or toasted sliced almonds

--------- ✿ ✿ ✿ ---------

In a large bowl, combine 1 1/2 cups flour and the salt. Add the eggs and stir until well blended. Turn the dough out onto a lightly floured board and knead until smooth, about 5 minutes; add a little more flour if the dough seems sticky.

Shape the dough into a ball. Cover the dough with an overturned bowl. Let rest for 30 minutes.

Cut the dough into 8 pieces. Roll one piece under your palms into a 1/2-inch-thick rope. Cut the rope into 1/2-inch pieces. If the dough feels sticky, use a tiny bit of flour to dust the board or your hands—don't coat with flour, or the oil will foam up when you fry the struffoli.

Pour about 2 inches oil into a deep heavy saucepan or a deep fryer. Heat the oil to 370°F on a deep-frying thermometer, or until a small bit of the dough dropped into the oil sizzles, swims rapidly around the pan, and turns brown in 1 minute.

Being careful not to splash the hot oil, slip just enough of the pieces of dough into the pan as will fit without crowding. Cook, stirring once or twice, until the struffoli are crisp and evenly golden brown, 1 to 2 minutes. Remove the struffoli with a slotted spoon and drain on paper towels. Continue with the remaining dough.

When all of the struffoli are fried, gently heat the honey just to a simmer in a large shallow saucepan. Remove from the heat, add the struffoli, and stir well. Pile the struffoli on a serving plate. Decorate with the candied fruits, sprinkles, or nuts.

These keep well covered at room temperature for several days. To serve, break off portions of the struffoli with two large spoons or a salad server.

CORRADO SOPRANO, JR.

CHAPTER TWO

The Soprano Family Tradition

A CONVERSATION WITH CORRADO SOPRANO, JR.

The reigning patriarch of the Soprano family is Corrado Soprano, Jr., known to all as simply Junior or "Uncle Jun'." Now in his 70s, Uncle Jun', like my parents, grew up in the First Ward of Newark surrounded by industrious, life-loving immigrants, mostly from the same neck of the Italian woods. His father, Corrado, Sr., was a stonemason and his mother, Mariangela, kept house in a walk-up tenement flat. It is wonderful to have Junior's eyewitness account of what it was like when Newark's Little Italy really was a little version of Italy.

These verbatim comments come from an interview with Mr. Soprano at his present home in Belleville. ✿

What was it like? I'll tell you what it was like. It was Valhalla. It was the Golden Age of Life. My brother, Johnny, and I had what you might call carte blanche to go anywhere and do anything in the neighborhood and we had a great time. We'd steal garlic from the vegetable peddler on the street and throw them at people we didn't like. We'd sneak into the back door of social clubs and watch. Did you know there were musicians who used to stroll up and down Garside Street? It was wonderful, I tell you, like an Italian Disneyland. Everybody knew everybody.

Of course, most people were poor working slobs and there was a lot of drinking and a lot of

domestic fights where some guy would crack his wife one and cops would come and drag him away, but that just added to the excitement. See, everyone was of the same, you know, socioeconomic level at that time, so people didn't feel so bad about it. Of course, there were some successful entrepreneurs in the neighborhood who had more wealth. Everyone looked up to them. They were called "men of respect."

The only time we *had* to be home, no ifs, ands, or buts, was at dinnertime. My old man would come in after cutting stone all day and he wanted his dinner on the table right at six o'clock, and if everyone wasn't sitting in their place, there would be hell to pay, my friend. The old man was not what you would call the gregarious type. He worked his butt off six days a week, twelve hours a day, and outside, too, in the rain and snow, a miserable g-d job. When he came home, he was beat. If he said anything, it was about being forced to keep working after smashing his finger, or how much he hated that prick, Gaetano the *padrone,* a Sigilian'. Or wondering why the Italian people always got the short end of the stick.

But Mama was a great cook, and she used to spend all day going

from one little shop to another getting the stuff for a good dinner. She'd wait for the vegetable peddler and his horse, Doxsie, to get broccoli and eggplant, then go to Dellacroche's Bakery to get bread, then to the pork store for meat, and Old Man Nunzio's for coffee. There was a macaroni factory nearby that would bring the macaroni right to your door. They brought ice that way too. And pizza peddlers on the streets, just like in Naples. For like pennies, you could get a slice whenever you wanted. It was wonderful, I tell you. I burnt the roof of my mouth very badly one time.

Mama always cooked. We never went out to eat, except to your Dad's place sometimes. Every dinner was something. In the winter it would be *pasta fazool* or *'shcarole* and beans. In the summer she'd switch to *giambott'* (with seasonal vegetables) or stuffed peppers. We ate like elephants, I tell you, but never got fat, except for Mama, of course. And no one died of too much cholesterol or some such crap. My brother, Johnny, God love him, succumbed to emphysema and cancer because of smoking too much. My father died of old age and bitterness. He just wore out one day and died.

Except for the old man, we all told stories while we ate, especially Johnny, who could spin 20 minutes of bullshit about a

three-minute walk to the corner. The best times we ever had was stuffing macaroni in our face and laughing at Johnny's stories, like the guy across the hall, D'Innocenzio, being cuckolded by his wife and Fascio the vegetable guy. Or the degenerate bastards Johnny was always beating at craps. We also had fun at all the religious feasts they used to have in the neighborhood, but that was just Johnny and me. The old man never went—he just stayed home and drank. *"Sputa sui santi,"* he used to say.

I miss those dinners, I guess, but what I really miss is my brother, Johnny. He was the life of the party. He made growing up fun.

Pasta Fagioli

Pasta Fazool——ᨑ——Pasta and Beans

Serves 8

8 ounces (1 cup) dried cannellini or Great Northern beans or 3 cups canned
　beans, rinsed and drained
1 celery rib, chopped
2 garlic cloves, lightly crushed
1/4 cup olive oil
1 cup peeled, seeded, and chopped fresh tomatoes or canned Italian peeled
　tomatoes
1 teaspoon tomato paste
1/2 cup water
1 small dried peperoncino, crumbled, or pinch of crushed red pepper
Salt
8 ounces ditalini or spaghetti or other pasta broken into 1-inch pieces

———————— ✦ ✦ ✦ ————————

If using dried beans, put them in a bowl with cold water to cover by 1 inch, and let stand for at least 4 hours, or overnight, in the refrigerator. Add more water if necessary to keep the beans covered.

Drain the beans and place them in a pot with fresh water to cover by 1/2 inch. Bring to a simmer over low heat. Cover the pot and cook until the beans are very soft, about 1 hour. Add more water if needed to keep the beans just covered. (You can substitute 3 cups canned beans, rinsed and drained.)

When the beans are almost ready, cook the celery and garlic in the olive oil in a large saucepan over moderate heat. When the garlic is golden, discard it. Add the tomatoes, tomato paste, water, peperoncino, and salt to taste. Simmer for 10 minutes, or until the sauce is slightly thickened.

Add the beans and their cooking liquid, or the canned beans, to the tomato sauce. Bring the mixture to a simmer, mashing some of the beans with the back of a large spoon.

Stir in the pasta and cook, stirring often, until the pasta is al dente, tender yet still firm to the bite. The mixture should be very thick, but add a little boiling water if it seems too thick. Turn off the heat and let stand for 10 minutes before serving.

Pasta e Patate

Pasta Padahn'——ⱳ——*Pasta and Potatoes*

Serves 6

2 thick slices pancetta or 4 slices bacon, chopped
1 small carrot, peeled and chopped
1 small celery rib, chopped
1 medium onion, chopped
1 garlic clove, very finely chopped
2 tablespoons chopped fresh flat-leaf parsley
2 tablespoons olive oil
1 tablespoon tomato paste
Salt and freshly ground pepper
1 1/2 pounds boiling potatoes, peeled and diced
6 cups water
12 ounces ditalini or small elbow macaroni
2 cups boiling water
1/2 cup freshly grated Pecorino Romano or Parmigiano-Reggiano

❖ ❖ ❖

Chop the pancetta, carrot, celery, onion, and parsley together. Pour the oil into a large saucepan, add the chopped mixture, and cook over medium-low heat until the vegetables are tender and golden.

Stir in the tomato paste and salt and pepper to taste. Add the potatoes and water, bring to a simmer, and cook until the potatoes are very tender, about 30 minutes. Mash some of the potatoes with the back of a spoon.

Add the pasta and boiling water. Cook, stirring often, until the pasta is tender. The mixture should remain quite thick, but add more water if it seems too thick.

Stir in the cheese and serve immediately.

Baccalà Pizzaiola

Baccalà Pizzaiol'—ᴡᴡ—Salt Cod Pizzamaker's Style

Serve 6 to 8

2 pounds baccalà (salt cod) or 1 1/2 pounds *pesce stocco* (stockfish)
6 tablespoons olive oil
2 large garlic cloves, very finely chopped
3 cups peeled, seeded, and chopped fresh tomatoes or one 28- to 35-ounce
   can Italian peeled tomatoes, drained and chopped
1 teaspoon dried oregano
Salt and freshly ground pepper
6 fresh basil leaves, torn into bits

☼ ☼ ☼

If using baccalà, place the fish in a large bowl with cold water to cover and place the bowl in the refrigerator to soak for 24 to 48 hours, changing the water every few hours, until the water no longer tastes salty.

If using stockfish, soak the fish in the same manner for 5 to 7 days, until it is soft and pliable.

Bring about 2 inches of water to a simmer in a deep skillet. Add the fish and cook for 10 minutes, or until it is tender but not breaking apart. Remove the fish with a slotted spoon. Let cool, then remove any skin and bones.

Meanwhile, put 1/4 cup of the oil in a medium saucepan with the garlic and cook over medium heat until the garlic is lightly golden. Add the tomatoes and their juice, the oregano, and salt and pepper to taste. Bring to a simmer and cook for 20 minutes or until the sauce is slightly thickened. Stir in the basil.

Preheat the oven to 400°F.

Choose a baking dish large enough to hold the fish in a single layer. Spoon a thin layer of sauce into the dish. Arrange the fish on top. Spoon on the remaining sauce and drizzle with the remaining 2 tablespoons oil.

Bake 30 minutes, or until the sauce is bubbling. Serve hot.

Rigatoni with Broccoli

—◊◊◊—

Serves 4
1 bunch broccoli (about 1 1/4 pounds)
Salt
1/4 cup olive oil
4 garlic cloves, thinly sliced
Pinch of crushed red pepper
8 ounces rigatoni
1/2 cup freshly grated Pecorino Romano or Parmigiano-Reggiano

—————— ✿ ✿ ✿ ——————

Trim the broccoli and cut it into bite-sized pieces. Bring 4 quarts of cold water to a boil in a large pot. Add the broccoli and salt to taste. Cook for 5 minutes. Scoop out the broccoli with a small sieve. Reserve the cooking water in the pot.

Pour the oil into a skillet large enough to hold all the ingredients. Add the garlic and red pepper and cook over medium heat for about 2 minutes, or until the garlic is lightly golden. Add the broccoli and a pinch of salt. Cook, stirring occasionally, for 10 minutes, or until the broccoli is very soft.

Meanwhile, bring the water back to a boil. Add the rigatoni and cook, stirring frequently, until the pasta is not quite tender. Scoop out about 1 cup of the cooking water and set it aside. Drain the rigatoni and add it to the skillet with the broccoli. Add the reserved cooking water and cook, stirring often, for 5 minutes more.

Sprinkle with the cheese, toss, and serve immediately.

Giambotta

Giambott' ⎯⎯⋙⎯⎯ *Vegetable Stew*

Serves 8

2 medium red bell peppers, cored, seeded, and cut into bite-sized pieces
2 large tomatoes, cored and cut into small pieces
2 medium potatoes, peeled and cut into bite-sized pieces
1 medium eggplant, cut into bite-sized pieces
1 large onion, diced
Salt and freshly ground pepper to taste
1/4 cup water
2 tablespoons olive oil
4 or 5 fresh basil leaves, torn into pieces

⎯⎯⎯⎯⎯⎯ ◊ ◊ ◊ ⎯⎯⎯⎯⎯⎯

In a large pot, combine all of the ingredients except the basil. Cover and cook, stirring occasionally, for about 30 minutes, until the vegetables are very tender.

Remove from the heat and stir in the basil. Serve hot or at room temperature.

Panzerotti

Panzerott'  *—Neapolitan Potato Croquettes*

Makes about 24

6 large boiling potatoes
3 large eggs, separated
1 cup freshly grated Pecorino Romano or Parmigiano-Reggiano
1/4 cup very finely chopped salami (about 2 ounces)
2 tablespoons chopped fresh flat-leaf parsley
Pinch of ground nutmeg
Salt and freshly ground pepper
About 2 cups plain bread crumbs, preferably homemade
Vegetable oil for shallow-frying

——————— ✿ ✿ ✿ ———————

Place the potatoes in a large saucepan with cold water to cover. Cover the pan, bring the water to a boil, and cook over medium heat for 30 minutes until the potatoes are tender when pierced with a fork. Peel the potatoes and mash them very, very fine. Let cool slightly.

Stir the egg yolks, cheese, salami, parsley, and nutmeg into the potatoes. Add salt and pepper to taste.

In a shallow dish, beat the egg whites until frothy. Spread the bread crumbs on a sheet of wax paper.

Using about 1/4 cup of the potato mixture, form it into a sausage shape about 1 inch thick and 2 1/2 inches long. Repeat with the remaining potato mixture.

Dip the potato logs into the egg whites, then roll them in the crumbs, coating them completely. Place the logs on a wire rack and let dry for 15 to 30 minutes.

Pour about 1/2 inch of oil into a large heavy skillet. Heat over medium heat until a bread crumb or a bit of the egg white sizzles when dropped in the oil. Place only enough of the logs in the pan as will fit without crowding—leave at least 1/2 inch space between them. Fry them, turning occasionally, until evenly browned. Drain the panzerott' on paper towels.

Serve immediately, or keep them warm in a low oven while you fry the remainder.

JANICE SOPRANO

CHAPTER THREE

Sunday Dinner

AS REMEMBERED BY JANICE SOPRANO

*J*anice Soprano is the oldest sibling in the Soprano family. She is of my generation, sister to Tony and the baby of the family, Barbara. Janice is a freelance artist and song composer. At the time of this writing, she lived in Seattle, Washington, where she was also employed in the food service industry. I asked her what Sunday dinner was like growing up in the Soprano home in West Orange. What follows is her audiotaped remembrance. ✿

Childhood is like a dream, isn't it, a distant, fog-strewn fantasy that we relive in the smallest of effluvia that drifts through our lives. We pick up a *biscotti al cioccolato* and are instantly transported back to Grandma's house where a skinned knee is magically healed with no more than a biscuit and a pat on the hindside. Or open a package of prosciutto and suddenly you're sweet sixteen, in your parent's bedroom, and Johnny Intili is snacking on *prozhoot'* and trying to unsnap your bra strap at the same time. When I dream, frankly, there is always food in there. It's the burden of being Italian.

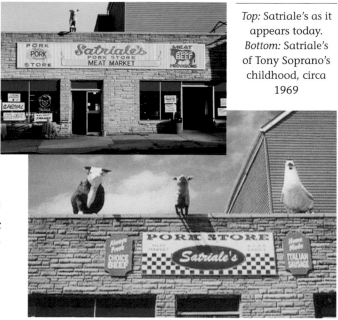

Top: Satriale's as it appears today. *Bottom:* Satriale's of Tony Soprano's childhood, circa 1969

I grew up in a typical Italian-American family of that era and milieu. My father, Giovanni, or Johnny, a strikingly handsome man, juggled the balls of many businesses. Through wise business practices, he became a partner in retail meats, specifically, Satriale's

Johnny and Livia Soprano, circa 1969.

Market, which meant that we always ate the best in pork and provisions.

My mother, Livia Pollio Soprano, was a typical stay-at-home mom, and her main job in life was to watch out for my father, "to protect him," she often said, "from the snakes." To me, he didn't seem to need protecting, but Ma was Ma. Of course, women today do not serve men as they did in those "dark ages," but this is what she knew. I don't think she liked the

backup role, but this may be the projection of an independent, world-savvy daughter who's had the advantages of travel and literature.

Sunday dinner was *the* time of the week for our little family. I always tried to help Ma with food preparation, but she usually brushed me aside with, "You'll eat half of it before it gets to the table." That was Ma's sense of humor—she'd try to get your goat at every turn.

I was in charge of setting the table, given the artistic touch that I, alone among my siblings, possess. My specialty was napkin flowers, an Oriental touch. Ma was too busy to notice and Daddy usually grabbed the napkin flower and stuffed it into his lap without looking. It was always his

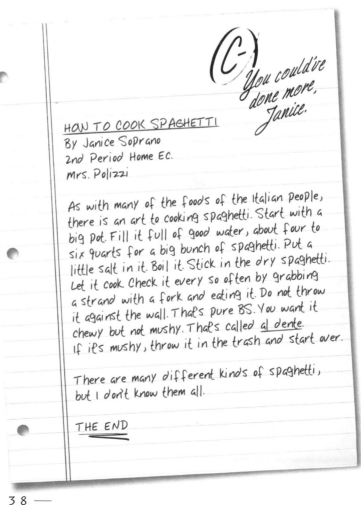

(C-)
You could've done more, Janice.

HOW TO COOK SPAGHETTI
By Janice Soprano
2nd Period Home Ec.
Mrs. Polizzi

As with many of the foods of the Italian people, there is an art to cooking spaghetti. Start with a big pot. Fill it full of good water, about four to six quarts for a big bunch of spaghetti. Put a little salt in it. Boil it. Stick in the dry spaghetti. Let it cook. Check it every so often by grabbing a strand with a fork and eating it. Do not throw it against the wall. That's pure BS. You want it chewy but not mushy. That's called al dente. If it's mushy, throw it in the trash and start over.

There are many different kinds of spaghetti, but I don't know them all.

THE END

Mushrooms
Romano''
Mozarell'
Ricotta
✓ Pork shoulder (Johnny)
Cipollini
Dutch Girl cleanser
✓ Basil
~~Vapo Rub~~
Zucchini
Baking powder
    (Arm & Hammer!)
Rigaton'
Salt—the Morton's
Gabagool (Anthony)
✓ Anchovies
~~TP~~
Kleenex
Tomatoes
Oil of Olay
Brioschi
Pecan Sandies
Batteries
    (flashlight type)
~~American bread~~
Italian bread
Chicken pot pie
Pudding for Janice
    Rice Krispies
Tang
    Dolly Madison cake

Thank YOU for your Prompt Payment!

Did You Remember to:
■ Sign your check?
■ Enclose the top portion of your bill with your check?
■ Write your account number on your payment?

booming voice that announced, "Pigs at the trough, now!" Being the spiritual one in the family, I said the blessing, and then the eating and the verbal jousting would commence. If you were a non-Italian fly on the wall, it probably sounded more like bickering than jousting. So be it. In my house, to love, to *care,* was to bicker, and vice versa.

The first topic was always Ma's inquiry into Daddy's business week. She knew where every nickel was buried. During these discussions, Daddy would often eat and smoke at the same time. Tony would then mention that he had seen Daddy helping Gloria Esposito with her groceries, which elicited a Ma comeback like, "Eat your broccoli, Anthony, and speak when you're spoken to."

Ma would always comment about my portion size and make an askew mention of my "ever-expanding backside." Tony, of course, would take even more food and no one said a thing. "Anthony," Ma would say, "doesn't have to fit into a prom dress." Daddy, for fun, would start in on the food. If the pork shoulder was overcooked (as always—Ma was terrified of trichinosis), he'd hold up a piece and announce today's special—"Particle Board à la Livia." Ma would say it's the only safe way to eat pork in this day and age, which Daddy would take as an indictment of his retail meat business, and the fur would fly. Always the kidder, Tony would stand and toss me a slice of bone-dry pork like a Frisbee, at which point Daddy would pull off his belt and tell him to "sit the f**k down."

My Recipe

BISCOTTI REGINA

Preheat the oven to 375°F. Butter and flour two large baking sheets. Pour the milk into a shallow bowl. Spread the sesame seeds on a piece of waxed paper. Set aside. In the bowl of a large electric mixer, stir together the flour, sugar, baking powder and salt. On low speed, beat in the butter a little at a time. In a medium bowl, whisk the eggs, vanilla, and orange zest. Stir the egg mixture into the dry ingredients until well blended. Pinch off a piece of dough the size of a golf ball and shape it into a log 2 1/2 inches long and 3/4 inch wide. Dip the log in the milk, then roll it in the sesame seeds. Place on a prepared baking sheet and flatten slightly. Continue with the remaining dough, placing the pieces about 1-inch apart. Bake 25 to 30 minutes or until well browned. Let cool on the baking sheet for 10 minutes, then transfer the cookies to a rack to cool completely. Store in an airtight container.

MAKES 50
1/2 cup milk
2 cups unhulled sesame seeds
4 cups all purpose flour
1 cup sugar
3-1/2 teaspoons baking powder
1/2 teaspoon salt
1/2 pound unsalted butter, cut into pieces and softened
2 large eggs, at room temperature
1 teaspoon vanilla extract
1 teaspoon grated orange zest

About this time, the phone would ring and it was usually one of Daddy's clients—and by the tone of his voice you could tell that a payment was not forthcoming. Being the family conciliator, I'd try to humor him, but he would stay focused on the food, much to Ma's chagrin. Tony would complain of a bellyache, which put Ma over the line. "Go eat at Bucco's!" she'd shout as she left the room in tears. "I give my children my life on a silver platter and all I hear is complaining!"

Daddy would curse, gulp down another glass of wine, and head upstairs to deal with Ma. Tony, not feeling well, would lie down on the couch and flick on bowling. Barbara would slip away to her room and it was thus left to me to clear the dishes, as usual, and pick apart what remained of the dehydrated pork, etc.

Before I got to the homemade biscotti, the shouting from above would subside and we knew that Ma and Daddy had made up and in fifteen minutes they'd be down. We'd all take a deep breath. Another Soprano Sunday dinner had come to a climactic—and life affirming—finale.

Dear Settima,

I know I haven't written in a while, but what with three underfoot incl. a 3-year-old, housework, cooking, etc., who has the time? We used to have fun, me and Johnny, but now it's just fix dinner, clean up vomit, spank Janice, etc. Every day I dream of getting out of this apt. & into a _real_ house. Johnny wants to move to Reno, Nevada, but I told him over my dead body. He's a dreamer. Me, I just want a gas oven that doesn't explode and an icebox that doesn't leak. Is that asking so much? →

Letter from Livia to
her sister Settima.

Janice's Vegetarian Baked Ziti

—◇◇◇—

Serves 6 to 8

For the Sauce
One 10-ounce package white mushrooms, trimmed
1 large onion, chopped
1/4 cup olive oil
2 garlic cloves, chopped
Two 28-ounce cans tomato puree
4 basil leaves torn into bits
Salt and freshly ground pepper
1 cup fresh or frozen peas

1 pound ziti
Salt
1 cup freshly grated Pecorino Romano or Parmigiano-Reggiano
1 cup ricotta
8 ounces mozzarella, cut into small dice

✿ ✿ ✿

Place the mushrooms in a colander and rinse them quickly under cold running water. (Do not soak mushrooms, or they will absorb too much water.) Drain the mushrooms and pat dry. Slice the mushrooms 1/4 inch thick.

To make the sauce, cook the onion in the oil in a large skillet until tender and golden. Stir in the mushrooms and garlic and cook until the mushrooms are lightly browned, about 10 minutes. Add the tomato puree, basil, and salt and pepper to taste. Bring to a simmer and cook for 30 minutes. Stir in the peas.

Meanwhile, bring at least 4 quarts of water to a boil in a large pot. Add the ziti and salt to taste. Cook, stirring frequently, until the pasta is al dente, tender yet firm to the bite.

Drain the ziti and place it in a bowl. Toss it with about 3 cups of the sauce and 3/4 cup of the grated cheese.

Preheat the oven to 350°F.

Spoon half the ziti into a shallow 3 1/2-quart baking dish. Spread the ricotta on top. Pour on 1 more cup of the sauce and sprinkle with the mozzarella. Top with the remaining ziti, sauce, and grated cheese. Cover the dish with foil. (The ziti can be refrigerated for several hours, or overnight, at this point. Remove from the refrigerator about 30 minutes before baking.)

Bake the ziti for 45 minutes. Uncover and bake for 15 to 30 minutes longer, or until the center is hot and the sauce is bubbling around the edges. Cover and let stand for 15 minutes before serving.

Livia's Fried Mushrooms

—∿—

Serves 4

One 10- to 12-ounce package white mushrooms, trimmed
1/4 cup olive oil
2 tablespoons chopped fresh flat-leaf parsley
2 large garlic cloves, thinly sliced
Salt and freshly ground pepper

——————— ✿ ✿ ✿ ———————

Place the mushrooms in a colander and rinse them quickly under cold running water. (Do not soak mushrooms, or they will absorb too much water.) Drain the mushrooms and pat them dry. Cut the mushrooms in half, or into quarters if large.

In a large skillet, heat the oil over medium heat. Add the mushrooms and cook, stirring often, until browned, 8 to 10 minutes. Sprinkle with the parsley, garlic, and salt and pepper to taste. Cook 2 minutes more, or until the garlic is golden. Serve hot.

Chicken Soup with Orzo

Serves 6
One 4-pound chicken
1 pound chicken backs and wings
2 medium carrots, chopped
2 celery ribs, chopped
2 onions, chopped
6 sprigs flat-leaf parsley
6 whole black peppercorns
Salt
8 ounces orzo or other small pasta, cooked

Rinse the chicken and chicken parts well. Set aside the giblets for another use. Place the chicken and chicken parts in a 6-quart pot. Add cold water to cover and bring to a simmer over medium heat. Reduce the heat to low and cook for 30 minutes. Skim off the foam and fat that rises to the surface.

Add the vegetables, parsley, peppercorns, and a little salt. Simmer for 1 1/2 hours or until the chicken is tender. Add more water if needed to keep the chicken submerged.

Remove the chicken from the pot; set the pot aside. Discard the skin and bones and cut the chicken into bite-sized pieces. Return the meat to the pot. Reheat gently.

Add the orzo, taste for seasoning, and serve hot.

Roasted Pepper Salad

—m—

Serves 8
8 large red, yellow, or green bell peppers
1/3 cup extra virgin olive oil
6 fresh basil leaves, torn into pieces, or 1 teaspoon dried oregano
2 garlic cloves, thinly sliced
Salt and freshly ground pepper

❈ ❈ ❈

Cover the broiler pan with foil. Place the peppers on the pan and place in the broiler so that the peppers are about 3 inches from the heat. Turn on the broiler to high. Broil the peppers, turning them frequently, until the skin blisters and they are charred all over. Put the peppers in a bowl, cover with foil, and let cool.

Cut the peppers in half, draining the juices into a bowl. Peel off the skin and discard the seeds and stems. Cut the peppers lengthwise into 1-inch strips and place in a serving bowl. Strain the juices over the peppers.

Add the olive oil, basil, garlic, and salt and pepper to taste. Let marinate for at least 30 minutes before serving.

Roast Pork Shoulder

—◊◊◊—

Serves 8 to 10
8 garlic cloves
1 tablespoon chopped fresh rosemary
1 tablespoon salt
1 teaspoon coarsely ground pepper
Olive oil
One 6-pound pork shoulder roast

———— ✿ ✿ ✿ ————

Preheat the oven to 350°F.

Finely chop the garlic and rosemary together. In a small bowl, mix together the chopped ingredients, the salt, pepper, and enough olive oil to form a paste.

With a small sharp knife, score the pork skin, cutting 1/4-inch-deep crosshatch lines. Poke deep pockets into the surface of the pork with the knife. Rub the paste into the cuts.

Place the pork in a large roasting pan. Roast for 3 hours. Tip the pan and carefully remove the excess fat.

Roast the meat for 1 1/2 to 2 hours longer, or until the skin is crisp and a deep nutty brown. Let stand for 20 minutes.

Remove the pork skin and cut into small pieces. Slice the meat. Serve the meat hot or at room temperature, with some of the pork skin.

Standing Rib Roast

—〰—

Serves 10

One 4-rib fully trimmed beef roast (about 8 pounds)
Salt and freshly ground pepper
2 medium carrots, peeled and cut into chunks
2 onions, cut into wedges
2 cups beef broth

————— ❖ ❖ ❖ —————

Preheat the oven to 325°F.

Place the meat fat side up in a large roasting pan. Sprinkle it all over with salt and pepper. Scatter the carrots and onions around the meat.

Place the roast in the lower third of the oven. Roast for 12 minutes to the pound for rare beef. An 8-pound roast will need about 1 hour and 45 minutes; the temperature of the meat should be 120° to 125°F on an instant-read thermometer.

Roast a little longer for medium-rare. (The USDA recommends cooking meat to 145°F, at which point it will be well-done.)

Transfer the meat to a cutting board. Cover with foil and let stand for 20 to 30 minutes.

Meanwhile, spoon off the fat in the roasting pan. Add the beef broth to the pan and place it over medium heat. Cook, scraping up browned bits in the bottom of the pan with a wooden spoon, for several minutes until slightly reduced. Strain the juices into a heated gravy boat.

Carve the meat and serve with the juices.

Manicotti

Manicott'

—◊◊◊—

Serves 6 to 8

For the Crepes
1 cup all-purpose flour
1 cup water
3 large eggs
1/2 teaspoon salt
Vegetable oil

For the Filling
2 pounds ricotta
4 ounces fresh mozzarella, chopped or shredded
1/2 cup freshly grated Parmigiano-Reggiano or Pecorino Romano
1 large egg
2 tablespoons chopped fresh flat-leaf parsley
Pinch of salt
Freshly ground pepper

Marinara Sauce (page 13), or Sunday Gravy (page 14)
1/2 cup freshly grated Parmigiano-Reggiano or Pecorino Romano

✿ ✿ ✿

To make the crepes, in a large bowl, whisk together the ingredients until smooth. Cover and refrigerate for at least 30 minutes.

Heat a 6-inch nonstick skillet or omelet pan over medium heat. Brush the pan lightly with oil. Holding the pan in one hand, spoon in about 1/3 cup of the crepe batter and immediately rotate and tilt the pan to completely cover the bottom. Pour any excess batter back into the bowl. Cook the crepe for 1 minute, or until the edges turn brown and begin to lift away from the pan. With your fingers, flip the crepe over, and cook for 30 seconds more, or until spotted with brown on the other side.

Slide the cooked crepe onto a plate. Cover with a piece of wax paper. Repeat with the remaining batter, stacking the crepes and separating each one with a piece of wax paper. (The crepes can be made up to 2 days ahead of serving. Cover with plastic wrap and store in the refrigerator until ready to use.)

Preheat the oven to 350°F.

To make the filling, stir together all of the ingredients in a large bowl.

Spoon a thin layer of the sauce into a 13 x 9 x 2-inch baking dish. Place about 1/4 cup of the filling lengthwise down the center of a crepe, roll it up, and place it seam side down in the dish. Continue with the remaining crepes and filling, placing them close together. Spoon on the remaining sauce. Sprinkle with the cheese.

Bake for 30 to 45 minutes, or until the sauce is bubbling and the manicotti are heated through. Serve hot.

Cavatelli

Gavadeel'——ᴡᴡ——*Pasta Shells*

Serves 6 to 8
2 cups fine semolina flour
1 cup all-purpose flour, plus more for dusting
Salt
About 1 cup warm water
Sunday Gravy (page 14) or a double recipe of Marinara Sauce (page 13)
Freshly grated Parmigiano-Reggiano or Pecorino Romano for serving

———— ✿ ✿ ✿ ————

Stir together the two flours and 1 teaspoon salt in a bowl. Gradually add enough water to form a stiff dough. Turn the dough out onto a lightly floured surface. Knead the dough until it is smooth, about 2 minutes. Shape the dough into a ball and cover it with a bowl. Let rest for 30 minutes.

Lightly dust 2 or 3 large cookie sheets with flour.

Cut the dough into 8 pieces. Work with one piece at a time, keeping the remainder covered. On a lightly floured surface, roll the piece of dough into a 1/2-inch-thick rope. Cut the rope into 1/2-inch pieces.

Using a small knife with a dull blade and rounded tip, press your index finger against the side of the blade and flatten each piece of dough, pressing and dragging it slightly so that the dough curls around the tip of the knife to form a shell shape.

Spread the cavatelli on a prepared cookie sheet. Repeat with the remaining dough.

(If you are not using the cavatelli within an hour, place the pans in the freezer. When the pieces are firm, scoop them into a plastic bag and seal tightly. Freeze until ready to use. Do not thaw before cooking.)

To cook the cavatelli, bring at least 4 quarts of water to a boil in a large pot over high heat. Add the cavatelli and salt to taste. Cook, stirring occasionally, until the pasta is tender yet still slightly chewy.

Meanwhile, reheat the sauce.

Drain the cavatelli and pour them into a heated serving bowl. Add the sauce and serve immediately, with grated cheese.

Amaretti

Almond Macaroons

—✥—

Makes 36
One 8-ounce can almond paste
1 cup sugar
2 large egg whites, at room temperature
36 red or green candied cherries or whole almonds

———————— ✿ ✿ ✿ ————————

Preheat the oven to 350°F. Line two large baking sheets with parchment paper or foil.

In a food processor or the large bowl of an electric mixer, combine the almond paste and sugar. Process or beat until blended. Add the egg whites and process or beat until very smooth.

Scoop up 1 tablespoon of the batter and lightly roll it into a ball. Dampen your fingertips with cool water if necessary to prevent sticking. Place on a prepared baking sheet and repeat with the remaining batter, placing the balls about 1 inch apart on the baking sheets. Push a candied cherry or almond into the top of each cookie.

Bake for 18 to 20 minutes, or until the cookies are lightly browned. Let cool briefly on the baking sheets. With a thin metal spatula, transfer the cookies to wire racks to cool completely.

Store the cookies in airtight containers.

Biscotti Regina

Sesame Cookies

—◊◊◊—

Makes 50

1/2 cup milk
2 cups unhulled sesame seeds
4 cups all-purpose flour
1 cup sugar
3 1/2 teaspoons baking powder
1/2 teaspoon salt
1/2 pound (2 sticks) unsalted butter, cut into pieces and softened
2 large eggs, at room temperature
1 teaspoon vanilla extract
1 teaspoon grated orange zest

——————— ✿ ✿ ✿ ———————

Preheat the oven to 375°F. Butter and flour two large baking sheets.

Pour the milk into a shallow bowl. Spread the sesame seeds on a piece of wax paper. Set aside.

In the large bowl of an electric mixer, stir together the flour, sugar, baking powder, and salt. On low speed, beat in the butter a little at a time.

In a medium bowl, whisk the eggs, vanilla, and orange zest. Stir the egg mixture into the dry ingredients until well blended.

Pinch off a piece of dough the size of a golf ball and shape it into a log 2 1/2 inches long and 3/4 inch thick.

Dip the log in the milk, then roll it in the sesame seeds. Place on a prepared baking sheet and flatten slightly. Continue with the remaining dough, placing the cookies about 1 inch apart.

Bake for 25 to 30 minutes, or until well browned. Let cool on the baking sheets for 10 minutes, then transfer the cookies to a rack to cool completely. Store in an airtight container.

CARMELA SOPRANO

CHAPTER FOUR

Feeding My Family
A Chat with Carmela Soprano

Carmela Soprano is the wife of Tony and the mother of two children, Meadow, 19, a student at Columbia University, and Anthony, Jr., or AJ, 16, a high school sophomore. They live in a lovely home in North Caldwell, New Jersey. With all of her family and charitable duties, which are considerable, Carmela still has the time and inclination to cook as many dinners for her family as possible. Why is cooking at home so important to her? What does it say about her heritage? To find out, we sat down for a heart to heart.✿

ARTIE: Carmela, you are a woman who is monetarily comfortable, why don't you have someone come in and help with the meals?

CARMELA: You know, that never crossed my mind. First of all, I don't like strangers in my house, nor does Tony. I know it's very fashionable nowadays to order out gourmet or pop a frozen risotto in the micro, but that's not me. I love to cook. Call me old-fashioned, but I think cooking is one way—maybe the *best* way—of communicating to my family that I love and care for them.

ARTIE: You don't feel like a slave to the frying pan?

CARMELA: I feel like a slave to the *dishwasher* sometimes, but cooking is no hardship.

Hunter Scangarelo and Meadow Soprano

And our house is designed in the contemporary open format where the kitchen is the center of things. You can learn a lot about your kids when they bring their friends over and hang around the fridge.

ARTIE: Not to mention your husband.

CARMELA *(joking)*: I won't let my husband bring *his* friends over.

ARTIE: Did your mother cook?

CARMELA: Of course. All mothers *used* to cook. But my mother cooked in a slightly different way than I do. She was Sicilian, you know, and my father's family is from the province of Caserta, but having married Tony, I have become a native of Avellino—a born-again Avellinese. This is very important to him, where he comes from. In fact, I use more recipes from *his* ma than from my own! Actually, what difference does it make? It's all the same stuff—tomatoes, garlic, what have you. The food of the South.

ARTIE: Give me an example of a Sicilian dish that you wouldn't fix for Tony.

CARMELA: When I was growing up, we used to have *pasta con le sarde* once in a while. That's pasta with sardines, a classic Sicilian meal. This is not something Tony wants to see under his nose at mealtime. Me neither, frankly.

WHY I LIKE FOOD

There is nothing on the (planete) better than food. sp
Food is serious. Sleep is ok and "The Simpsons"
can get you laughing, but they dont hold a
candle to King Food. Food always hits the spot,
morning, noon or night. In the morning, three you're
Pop-Tarts and a swig of Coke. Noon chili fries kidding?!
and another Coke. After school, pizza; I'm big
sp on (carbohidrats.) Dinner, some manicotti fixed by
mia madre or even my grandma's baked ziti.
It's all good. Skip the (ardichokes) and the liver, sp
and it's all good.

I dont get how girls can eat squat to stay skinny.
It makes no sense. If you can't eat all the delicious
vague stuff that (god) has given us, what's the reason
for living? To look good for your boyfriend? Please.
I'm glad I'm not a girl, I'll tell you that. My coach
loves it when I eat like a pig. That's what makes
football a great sport. And food is what makes
life a great life.

My grandma once told me that I would die alone.
If I die alone with a full stomach, that's ok with me.

Very interesting!
Your diet is pathetic
but your writing is
much improved!

Anthony Soprano, Jr.
5th period
Room 106

C++

AJ on his favorite subject—food.

ARTIE: He'd rather see a nice *rigaton'* with sweet sausage and tomato.

CARMELA: Exactly. Or baked ziti, which was really the only complex dish his mother knew how to make.

ARTIE: How else would you describe your family cuisine?

CARMELA: Lots of vegetables. *'Shcarole,* of course. Fried zucchini flowers, for special occasions. Frozen spinach, which is as good as fresh. *'Shcarole* soup. I try to cook healthy.

ARTIE: Today's younger generation—how do they take to the traditional dishes?

CARMELA: Are you kidding? Italian food is so "in" with these kids. They read that Brad Pitt loves garlic or that Ally McBeal beanpole lives on primavera and they want the same thing. What's not to like? Of course AJ avoids the veggies and inhales pizza. And Meadow comes home from college just to grab *rigaton'* to take back with her. The calories are a concern to her, though. Me too!

"Don't Even Go There"
MEADOW E-MAIL ON FOOD & WEIGHT

Hollyweird [Hunter]: i **hate** food

Bella18681 [Meadow]: don't even go there

Holly: i'm goin on a fast

Bella: yeah, ok, sure

Holly: winona ryder did, said it was mind-blowing

Bella: cancel your subscrib to *People*

Holly: i'm thinking about that

Bella: i weigh a **ton**

Holly: you have an eatin disorder. you look fine

Bella: i wish i had a eating disorder

Holly: forget it. its all genetic.you are what you are

Bella: then i are a fatso full-figured mama for life??

Holly: **YOURE NOT FAT! GOD!** ☹

Bella: its bad eating habits growin up. what prof ravitch calls cellular conditioning. pasta. stogliatell. chees. olive oil. **Ddamn all fat** italians! wish ii was born japanese.

Holly: no u don't. u cant even speek the language.

Bella: i'm going bulmic.

Holly: like nan steen the throwup queen

Bella: the **skinny** throwup queen

Holly: ☺ LOL ☺

Bella: du u know how much fat is in one double cheesburg?

Holly: let me get a pencil.

Bella: 94 grams!..that's a week worth. U know how many fat cals in olive oil?

Holly: thought it was good for cancer

Bella: **its all fat cals!!!!!!**

Holly: **wow**

Bella: 3 pieces of bread soaked in olive oil is like eating **3 piecs of cheescake!**

Holly: theres a cheescake diet, u know…i read it in *People*

Bella: and you know that Ital. sausage my mom buys?

Holly: bter than curry & artichoke kind we eat

Bella: each one 822 cals **90% fattttttttttt** .greasyoilypukey**FAT**

Holly: stop going home

Bella: ii hate it when dad grabs my handle bars and goes "youre wasting away"

Holly: is that child abuse

Bella: its abuse all right but i'm not a child, you know. i can vote

Holly: that's scary

Bella: i'm crying now

Holly: why? voting's not that hard

Bella: cuz you brought up food & that's all i think about anyway and **i'm screwed.** look at my fat pop. **totally screwed.**

Holly: so sorry. lets talk school

Bella: too late. i'm eating licorice

Holly: lucky u

ARTIE: I don't think you have anything to worry about.

CARMELA: Aren't you nice!

ARTIE: Is dinner an important occasion in your family?

CARMELA: It may be the *only* family occasion, except for confirmations and funerals. Given Tony's odd hours and such, without a regular sit-down dinner, we'd only talk through Post-it notes on the fridge! Tony likes to grill on the weekends, so that keeps everyone around, too. He's an excellent grillmaster.

ARTIE: You do occasionally eat out, don't you?

CARMELA: Of course, Artie, eating out is important for the economy, right?

ARTIE: At least *my* economy.

CARMELA: And I know that Tony and I communicate better when we step out without distractions and share a private meal.

ARTIE: So, to sum up, food to you is much more than something to eat…

CARMELA: My own philosophy is that food is a language, Artie, a way of building bridges, of saying what can't be put into words. If someone were sick, would you send flowers or balloons? Many would, but my inclination would be to send over a *pastina* and ricotta. It's healing food.

ARTIE: And it's more personal, more *you.*

CARMELA: I once made a ricotta pie with pineapple to give to a local professional woman to do me an important favor. I thought it was a nice touch. She must have really enjoyed it—she came through so nicely.

Ricotta-Pineapple Pie

—✿—

Serves 8

1 tablespoon unsalted butter, softened
1/4 cup fine graham cracker crumbs
1/2 cup sugar
2 tablespoons cornstarch
One 15-ounce container ricotta
2 large eggs
1/2 cup heavy cream
1 teaspoon grated lemon zest
1 teaspoon vanilla extract

For the Topping
One 20-ounce can crushed pineapple in syrup
1/4 cup sugar
1 tablespoon cornstarch
2 teaspoons fresh lemon juice

✿ ✿ ✿

Preheat the oven to 350°F. Spread the butter over the bottom and sides of a 9-inch pie pan or springform pan. Add the crumbs, turning the pan to coat the bottom and sides.

In a large bowl, stir together the sugar and cornstarch. Add the ricotta, eggs, cream, lemon zest, and vanilla and beat until smooth. Pour the mixture into the prepared pan.

Bake for 50 minutes, or until the pie is set around the edges but the center is still slightly soft. Cool to room temperature on a wire rack.

To make the topping, drain the pineapple well, reserving 1/2 cup of the liquid. In a medium saucepan, stir together the sugar and cornstarch. Stir in the 1/2 cup pineapple juice and the lemon juice. Cook, stirring, until thickened, about 1 minute. Add the pineapple. Remove from the heat and let cool slightly.

Spread the pineapple mixture over the pie. Cover and chill for at least 1 hour before serving.

Minestra

Minest' —w— Escarole and Little Meatballs Soup

Serves 6

1 head escarole (about 1 pound)
6 quarts chicken broth, preferably homemade
3 large carrots, chopped

For the Meatballs

1 pound ground veal or beef
2 large eggs
1/2 cup very finely minced onion
1 cup plain bread crumbs
1 cup freshly grated Parmigiano-Reggiano
1 teaspoon salt
Freshly ground pepper to taste

8 ounces ditalini or tubetti, or spaghetti broken into bite-sized pieces
Freshly grated Parmigiano-Reggiano

——————— ❖ ❖ ❖ ———————

Trim the escarole and discard any bruised leaves. Cut off the stem ends. Separate the leaves and wash well in cool water, especially the center of the leaves where soil collects. Stack the leaves and cut them crosswise into 1-inch strips. You should have about 4 cups.

In a large pot, combine the escarole, broth, and carrots. Bring to a simmer and cook until the escarole is almost tender, about 30 minutes.

Meanwhile, mix together all of the meatball ingredients. Shape the mixture into tiny balls, less than 1 inch in diameter.

When the escarole is cooked, stir in the pasta and return the soup to the simmer. Drop the meatballs into the soup. Cook over low heat, stirring gently, until the meatballs and pasta are cooked, about 20 minutes. Taste for seasoning.

Serve hot with grated Parmesan.

Rigatoni with Sweet Sausage and Tomato Sauce

—᙭᙭—

Serves 6

1 pound plain Italian-style pork sausages
2 tablespoons olive oil
2 garlic cloves, finely chopped
1/2 cup dry white wine
3 pounds plum tomatoes, peeled, seeded, and chopped,
    or one 28- to 35-ounce can Italian peeled tomatoes,
    passed through a food mill
Salt and freshly ground pepper
3 or 4 fresh basil leaves, torn into bits
1 pound rigatoni
1/2 cup freshly grated Pecorino Romano

——————— ✿ ✿ ✿ ———————

Remove the sausage from the casings. Chop the meat fine.

In a large pot, heat the oil over medium heat. Add the sausage and garlic and cook, stirring frequently, until the sausage is lightly browned. Add the wine and bring to a simmer. Cook until most of the wine evaporates.

Stir in the tomatoes and salt and pepper to taste. Bring to a simmer. Reduce the heat to low and cook, stirring occasionally, until the sauce is thickened, 1 hour and 15 to 30 minutes. Stir in the basil.

Meanwhile, bring at least 4 quarts of water to a boil in a large pot over high heat. Add the rigatoni and salt to taste. Cook, stirring occasionally until the rigatoni is al dente, tender yet still firm to the bite. Drain.

In a large heated serving bowl, toss the rigatoni with the sauce. Serve with the grated cheese.

'Shcarole with Garlic

Sautéed Escarole

—∿—

Serves 4
1 head escarole (about 1 pound)
3 garlic cloves, thinly sliced
Pinch of crushed red pepper (optional)
3 tablespoons olive oil
Salt

———— ✿ ✿ ✿ ————

Trim the escarole and discard any bruised leaves. Cut off the stem ends. Separate the leaves and wash well in cool water, especially the center of the leaves where soil collects. Stack the leaves and cut them into bite-sized pieces.

In a large pot, cook the garlic and red pepper, if using, in the olive oil over medium heat until the garlic is golden. Add the escarole and salt to taste. Stir well. Cover the pot and cook until the escarole is tender, about 15 minutes.

Serve hot or at room temperature.

Ziti al Forno

Baked Ziti with Little Meatballs

—∽—

Serves 8 to 12

1 pound ziti

Salt

Sunday Gravy (page 14) made with little meatballs

1 cup freshly grated Pecorino Romano or Parmigiano-Reggiano

1 cup ricotta

8 ounces mozzarella, cut into small dice

——————— ✿ ✿ ✿ ———————

Bring at least 4 quarts of water to a boil in a large pot. Add the ziti and salt to taste. Cook, stirring frequently, until the ziti is al dente, tender yet firm to the bite.

Meanwhile, remove the meats, including the meatballs, from the gravy. Set the pork, veal, and sausage aside for the second course, or for another meal.

Drain the ziti and put it in a large bowl. Toss it with about 3 cups of the gravy and half the grated cheese. Stir in the meatballs.

Preheat the oven to 350°F.

Spoon half the ziti into a shallow 3 1/2-quart baking dish. Spread the ricotta on top and sprinkle with the mozzarella and half of the remaining grated cheese. Pour on 1 cup of the sauce. Top with the remaining ziti and another cup of sauce. Sprinkle with the remaining grated cheese. Cover the dish with foil. (The ziti can be refrigerated for several hours, or overnight, at this point. Remove from the refrigerator about 30 minutes before baking.)

Bake the ziti for 45 minutes. Uncover and bake for 15 to 30 minutes longer, or until the center is hot and the sauce is bubbling around the edges. Cover and let stand for 15 minutes before serving.

Baked Chicken with Potatoes, Lemon, and Oregano

—〜—

Serves 4

2 lemons

1 chicken (about 3 1/2 pounds), quartered

3 potatoes, peeled and cut into wedges

1 tablespoon olive oil

1 teaspoon dried oregano

2 garlic cloves, chopped

Salt and freshly ground pepper

——————— ✿ ✿ ✿ ———————

Preheat the oven to 450°F.

Squeeze the juice from 1 lemon. Slice the other one.

Put the chicken and potatoes in a baking pan large enough to hold them in a single layer. Sprinkle with the lemon juice, oil, oregano, garlic, and salt and pepper to taste. Turn the pieces to coat evenly, then turn the chicken skin side up. Tuck the lemon slices and potatoes in between the chicken pieces.

Bake the chicken for 45 minutes. Baste with the pan juices. Continue to bake, basting occasionally, for 15 to 30 minutes longer, or until the chicken is browned and the potatoes are tender.

Transfer the chicken, potatoes, and lemon slices to a serving platter. Tip the pan and skim off the fat. Pour the juices over the chicken and serve.

Pastina with Ricotta

—∽—

Serves 1 or 2

1/2 cup pastina
Salt
1/4 cup ricotta
1 teaspoon unsalted butter

——————— ✿ ✿ ✿ ———————

Bring about 4 cups water to a boil in a small saucepan. Add the pastina and salt to taste. Cook, stirring frequently, until the pastina is tender, about 5 minutes.

Scoop out some of the cooking water. Drain the pastina and place it in a bowl with the ricotta and butter. Mix well, adding a little of the cooking water if the pasta seems dry. Serve immediately.

Mom's Pear and Grappa Pound Cake

—m—

Serves 12

One 16-ounce can pear halves or slices
3 cups all-purpose flour
2 1/2 teaspoons baking powder
1/2 teaspoon salt
1/2 pound (2 sticks) unsalted butter, softened
1 1/2 cups sugar
3 large eggs
3 tablespoons grappa, rum, or brandy
1 teaspoon vanilla extract
Confectioners' sugar

✿ ✿ ✿

Preheat the oven to 350°F. Butter and flour a 10-inch Bundt pan or tube pan.

Drain the pears and reserve the liquid. Chop the pears into 1/2-inch pieces. You should have about 1 1/4 cups pears and 1/2 cup liquid.

In a medium bowl, stir together the flour, baking powder, and salt.

In the large bowl of an electric mixer, beat the butter and sugar on medium speed until light and fluffy, about 5 minutes. Add the eggs one at a time, beating well after each addition. Beat in the reserved pear liquid, the grappa, and vanilla. (The batter will look curdled.)

Reduce the speed to low. Add the flour mixture, scraping the sides of the bowl as necessary and beating just until blended, about 1 minute. With a rubber spatula, stir in the pears.

Scrape the batter into the prepared pan. Bake until the cake pulls away from the sides of the pan and a toothpick inserted in the center comes out clean, about 1 hour and 15 minutes. Cool in the pan on a wire rack for 10 minutes.

Invert the cake onto a rack and remove the pan. Let cool completely.

Sprinkle with confectioners' sugar before serving.

ARTIE BUCCO

CHAPTER FIVE

Mia Cucina

BY ARTIE BUCCO

And now I have the honor and pleasure of serving up some of my own culinary creations.

Cooking, needless to say, is my life, but it wasn't always that way. Having been raised in a family of restaurateurs, I rebelled in high school and couldn't stand the sight of spaghetti. I committed myself to a strict diet of chili burgers and Slim Jims. My dream was to move to Los Angeles and play electric bass for the heavy metal band Judas Priest. I got as far as Pittsburgh and ran out of money. And I was hungry for some manicott'.

I bused tables and washed dishes at my parents' place night and day to raise the cash to go to the prestigious Cooks Culinary Academy in London, England. (I found out later that Paris was also a culinary center.) In six months, I learned everything I could about international cuisine, but to know Weiner schnitzel is not necessarily to love Weiner schnitzel. I initially stuck with what got me there—my grandpa's rice balls—but I quickly learned that you could have your pasta and eat it too. People think I rode in on the Eighties Tuscan boom—shrimp and cannellini, steak florentina, etc.—but not so. I figured that you could stick with the old ways and still make them new with a deft and delicate touch of creativity. And thus was born my own style of traditional Italian cuisine—neotraditional. It's the same old food only different.

I remember my very first cook-off at the academy. Boy, was I a jumble of nerves. My competitors were not just brilliant young chefs from Scotland and Sweden, but also two native Neapolitans who brought their own homemade olive oil! What did I know? I was from Jersey and the closest I'd ever gotten to Naples at the time was watching Sophia Loren in "Marriage Italian-Style" on late-night TV. Still, my heart

Artie on Olive Oil

Olive oils are a bit like wine—they vary according to region, variety, and age. Southern Italian olive oils are very aromatic and good for blending. The best olive oils are extra virgin—they come from the first squeezing of the olives, are pressed without heat or chemicals, and have low acidic content. The better the oil, the lower the acidity level. There is also "light" olive oil, but it doesn't mean lower in calories. It means lighter in flavor.

beat Neapolitan, or more precisely, Avellinese, and somewhere I knew I could come up with something out of my gastronomic imagination to out-Italian the Italians.

And that dish, made in a moment of youthful desperation, is still served nightly at Nuovo Vesuvio—"Quail Sinatra-Style." My secret ingredient—sun-dried tomatoes. Sure, they originally came from "the Boot," but no one there much cared about them and I had read a great magazine article about the new California cuisine on the plane ride over. So a culinary tidbit that went from Sicily to Naples to California to Newark to London got me a third prize in my very first competition. First prize went to a Scottish concoction called "Haddock Mousse."

How did Quail Sinatra-Style gets its name? Frank was singing "Luck Be a Lady" on the 8-track when it came to me. I was way past Judas Priest by then.

By far my proudest moment was the first meal I served my parents after returning from London. I wanted to make a statement about my emerging neotraditional style, so I fixed a simple but daring dish that had never crossed their lips—pasta alla vodka. My mother hated it—it wasn't "our food," plus she had no love for the Russians. My father, on the other hand, gorged himself and immediately added the dish to the dinner menu, causing quite a stir among the regular clientele. It wasn't until he saw the college crowd gushing over it that he realized an important lesson of modern Italian cuisine— innovate or die.

I could tell you a hundred more stories about my life in food, but time is short and food is always better than talk. So, as Grandma used to inveigh, "Mangia, mangia!" *Eat and enjoy.*✿

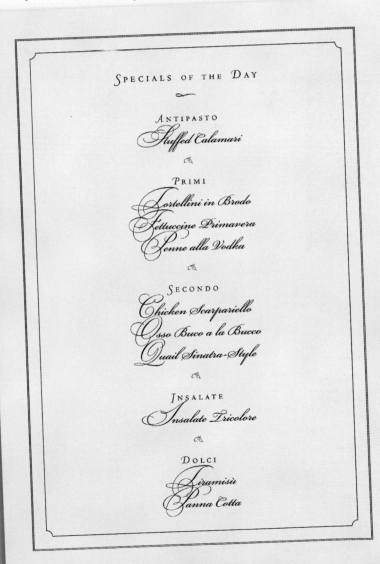

SPECIALS OF THE DAY

ANTIPASTO
Stuffed Calamari

PRIMI
Tortellini in Brodo
Fettuccine Primavera
Penne alla Vodka

SECONDO
Chicken Scarpariello
Osso Buco a la Bucco
Quail Sinatra-Style

INSALATE
Insalate Tricolore

DOLCI
Tiramisù
Panna Cotta

Artie on Wine Tips

Having attended a few "for professionals only" Wine Lovers Weekends in Atlantic City with the world-famous sommelier Charles Scicolone, I feel qualified to pass on my own preferences.

Southern Italy is the "new frontier" of Italian wines, especially the region of Campania, i.e., the greater Neapolitan area. For white wines specifically from Avellino, look for these names: Fiano di Avellino, Greco di Tufo, Lacrima Christi del Vesuvio, and Asperino di Aversa. For a great red wine from the area, look for a nice Taurasi or the red version of Lacrima Christi.

Of course, if it is your wont, you can go with California wines, or those from Northern Italy, or France! But if you want to feel like you're sitting in a corner caffè in Napoli chowing down on a little steak pizzaiol', try one of the above.

TODAY'S WINE SPECIAL

Lacrima Christi Del Vesuvio
(RED OR WHITE)

A tasteful "frutta della vigna" (fruit of the vineyard) from So. Italy. Translated, "Lacrima Christi" means "The Tears of Christ."

As the story goes, when the Archangel Lucifer was kicked out of heaven, he stole a piece of Paradise and dropped it in what is now the Bay of Naples. When Christ saw this, he cried. His tears landed on the slopes of Mt. Vesuvius and from these celestial tears came the classic grapes of Lacrima Christi.

Try it. You won't be disappointed.

Salut', Artie

Fettuccine Primavera

—∾—

Serves 6

4 tablespoons unsalted butter
1 small onion, finely chopped
2 medium carrots, peeled and finely diced
1 cup broccoli florets (cut into 3/4-inch pieces)
1 cup asparagus tips
1/2 cup fresh or frozen peas
1 cup heavy cream
Salt and freshly ground pepper
10 basil leaves, stacked and cut into thin ribbons
1 pound fresh fettuccine
3/4 cup freshly grated Parmigiano-Reggiano

————————— ✿ ✿ ✿ —————————

Bring at least 4 quarts of water to a boil in a large pot. Add salt to taste. Add the broccoli and asparagus and cook for 1 minute. With a small sieve, scoop out the vegetables and drain them well. Leave the water boiling in the pot.

In a skillet large enough to hold the cooked fettuccine, melt the butter over medium heat. Add the onion and carrots and cook, stirring occasionally, for 5 minutes, or until softened.

Add the broccoli and asparagus to the skillet, along with the peas and cream. Bring to a simmer. Season to taste with salt and pepper. Stir in the basil and turn off the heat.

Drop the fettuccine into the boiling water and cook, stirring frequently, until al dente, tender yet still firm to the bite. Drain the fettuccine and add it to the skillet. Add the cheese and toss well. Serve immediately.

Tortellini in Brodo

Tortellini in Broth

—◊◊—

Serves 8

For the Filling
2 tablespoons butter
4 ounces boneless pork loin, cut into 1-inch cubes
4 ounces prosciutto
4 ounces mortadella
1 cup freshly grated Parmigiano-Reggiano
1 large egg
1/4 teaspoon freshly ground nutmeg

For the Pasta
4 large eggs
1 tablespoon olive oil
About 3 cups all-purpose flour

To Serve
8 cups beef broth, preferably homemade
8 cups chicken broth, preferably homemade
Freshly grated Parmigiano-Reggiano

————— ✿ ✿ ✿ —————

To make the filling, melt the butter in a small skillet over medium heat. Add the pork and cook, stirring occasionally, until cooked through, about 20 minutes. Let cool.

In a food processor or meat grinder, grind the pork, prosciutto, and mortadella very fine. In a bowl, mix the ground meats with the Parmigiano, egg, and nutmeg. Cover and refrigerate until ready to use.

To make the pasta, put the eggs and oil in a food processor or the bowl of a heavy-duty mixer. Gradually add 2 1/2 cups of the flour and mix until the dough forms a ball. Stop the machine and feel the dough: it should be moist but not sticky. Add more flour if needed.

Transfer the dough to a lightly floured surface. Knead the dough for about 1 minute, until it feels firm and smooth. Cover with a bowl and let rest for 30 minutes.

Line 2 or 3 large baking sheets with lint-free towels. Dust the towels with flour.

Divide the dough into 8 pieces. Work with one piece at a time, keeping the remainder covered with the overturned bowl.

With a rolling pin or pasta machine, roll out the dough as thin as possible. Cut the dough into 2-inch squares. Place about 1/2 teaspoon of the filling on each square. Working quickly so that the dough does not dry out, fold the dough over the filling to form a triangle, and press the edges together to seal.

Fold the two opposite points of the triangle together, to form a circle, and pinch the ends to seal. Place the formed tortellini on a prepared baking sheet and prepare the remaining dough and filling in the same way.

Refrigerate the tortellini until ready to cook, up to several hours, or overnight. (For longer storage, freeze them on the baking sheets for 1 hour, or until firm, then transfer them to plastic bags and store in the freezer up to 1 month. Do not thaw before cooking.)

To serve, combine the beef and chicken broths in a large pot. Bring to a simmer. Add the tortellini and cook, stirring occasionally, 3 to 5 minutes or until the pasta is cooked through. Serve with grated Parmigiano-Reggiano.

Arancini

Arangeen'——m——*Rice Balls*

Makes 18

For the Filling
2 tablespoons olive oil
1 small onion, very finely chopped
1 garlic clove, finely chopped
8 ounces ground beef
1 1/2 cups chopped canned Italian peeled tomatoes
Salt and freshly ground pepper
1/2 cup frozen peas

For the Rice
5 cups chicken broth
1/2 teaspoon saffron threads, crumbled
2 cups (1 pound) medium-grain rice, such as Arborio
2 tablespoons butter
Salt
1/2 cup freshly grated Parmigiano-Reggiano
1/2 cup freshly grated Pecorino Romano
4 large egg yolks

To Assemble
5 large egg whites
2 cups plain bread crumbs
Flour for dredging
4 ounces sharp provolone, cut into small dice
Vegetable oil for deep-frying

————— ✧ ✧ ✧ —————

To make the filling, put the oil, onion, and garlic in a medium skillet, turn on the heat to medium, and cook until the onion is soft, about 5 minutes.

Add the beef to the skillet and cook, stirring to break up the lumps, until lightly browned, about 10 minutes. Stir in the tomatoes, and salt and pepper to taste. Bring the sauce to a simmer, reduce the heat to low, and cook, stirring occasionally, until thick, about 30 minutes.

Add the peas and cook 5 minutes more. Let cool.

To make the rice, bring the broth and saffron to a boil in a large pot. Stir in the rice, butter, and salt to taste. Cover, reduce the heat to low, and cook until the rice is tender, about 18 minutes.

Remove the rice from the heat and stir in the cheeses. Let cool slightly, then stir in the egg yolks.

To assemble, beat the egg whites in a shallow bowl until foamy. Spread the bread crumbs on one sheet of wax paper and the flour on another. Place a cake rack over a baking sheet.

Dip your hands in cool water, to prevent the rice from sticking. Scoop up about 1/3 cup of the rice mixture and place it in the palm of one hand. Poke a shallow hole in the center of the rice. Press about 1 tablespoon of the filling into the hole and top it with a piece of provolone. Cup your hand slightly, molding the rice over the filling to enclose it completely. Add a little more rice if necessary to cover the filling completely. Very gently squeeze the ball together to compact the rice.

Carefully roll the rice ball in the flour, then in the egg whites to coat it completely. Roll the ball in the bread crumbs, being sure not to leave any spots uncovered. Place the rice ball on the cake rack to dry. Continue making rice balls with the remaining ingredients, rinsing your hands between each. When all of the rice balls have been made, place the rack in the refrigerator for 30 minutes to dry.

Pour about 3 inches of oil into an electric deep-fryer or a deep heavy saucepan. Heat the oil until the temperature reaches 375°F on a deep-frying thermometer, or a drop of egg white sizzles when it is added to the oil. With a slotted spoon or skimmer, lower a few rice balls at a time into the hot oil; do not crowd the pan. Cook until golden brown and crisp all over, 3 to 4 minutes. Transfer the rice balls to paper towels to drain. Keep the cooked rice balls warm in a low oven while you fry the remainder. Serve hot or warm.

Penne alla Vodka

—✍—

Serves 4 to 6

3 tablespoons unsalted butter

2 large garlic cloves, finely chopped

2 ounces thinly sliced prosciutto, cut into thin strips

One 28- to 35-ounce can Italian peeled tomatoes, drained and coarsely
  chopped

1/2 teaspoon crushed red pepper

1/2 cup heavy cream

1/4 cup vodka

Salt

1 pound penne

1/2 cup freshly grated Parmigiano-Reggiano

✿ ✿ ✿

In a skillet large enough to hold the cooked pasta, melt the butter over medium heat. Add the garlic and cook until golden, about 2 minutes. Stir in the prosciutto and cook for 1 minute.

Add the tomatoes and crushed red pepper and simmer for 5 minutes. Stir in the cream and cook, stirring well, for 1 minute. Add the vodka and cook for 2 minutes. Season to taste with salt.

Meanwhile, bring at least 4 quarts of water to a boil in a large pot. Add the pasta and salt to taste. Cook, stirring frequently, until the penne is al dente, tender yet still firm to the bite. Drain the pasta, reserving some of the cooking water.

Add the pasta to the skillet with the sauce and toss the pasta until it is well coated. Add a little of the reserved cooking water if the sauce seems too thick. Add in the cheese and toss again. Serve immediately.

Ravioli alla Bucco

—◊◊◊—

Serves 8

For the Pasta
3 large eggs, beaten
1/4 cup cool water
1 teaspoon olive oil
About 3 cups all-purpose flour

For the Filling
1 pound whole-milk ricotta
4 ounces fresh mozzarella, coarsely grated or very finely chopped
4 ounces prosciutto, finely chopped
1 large egg
1/2 cup freshly grated Parmigiano-Reggiano
2 tablespoons chopped fresh flat-leaf parsley
Salt and freshly ground pepper to taste

To Serve
Sunday Gravy (page 14) or double recipe Marinara Sauce (page 13)
1 cup freshly grated Parmigiano-Reggiano

✿ ✿ ✿

To make the pasta, put the eggs, water, and oil in a food processor or the bowl of a heavy-duty mixer. Gradually add about 2 1/2 cups flour and mix until the dough forms a ball. Stop the machine and feel the dough: it should be moist but not sticky. Add more flour if needed.

Transfer the dough to a lightly floured surface. Knead the dough for about 1 minute, until it feels firm and smooth. Shape the dough into a ball. Cover with a bowl and let rest for 30 minutes.

To make the filling, mix together all of the ingredients in a bowl. Cover and refrigerate.

Line 2 or 3 large baking sheets with lint-free towels. Dust the towels with flour.

Cut the dough into 8 pieces. Work with one piece at a time, leaving the remaining pieces covered.

Shape the piece of dough into a flat disk. Lightly dust the rollers of a pasta machine

with flour. Set the rollers at the widest opening. Pass the dough through the machine. Set the rollers to the next setting and pass the dough through the machine. Continue to pass the dough through each successive setting until it is very thin and you reach the last or second-to-the-last setting, depending on your pasta machine. If the dough sticks or tears, dust it with flour, fold it, and pass it through the machine again.

Lay the strip of dough on a lightly floured surface. Fold it lengthwise in half to mark the center, then unfold it. Beginning about 1 inch from one of the short ends, place teaspoonfuls of the filling about 1 inch apart in a straight row down one side of the fold. Lightly brush around the mounds of filling with cool water. Fold the dough over the filling. Press out any air bubbles and seal the edges. Use a fluted pastry wheel or a sharp knife to cut between the mounds of filling. Separate the ravioli and press the edges firmly with a fork to seal. Place the ravioli in a single layer on a prepared baking sheet.

Repeat with the remaining dough and filling. Cover the ravioli with a towel and refrigerate until ready to cook, or up to 3 hours, turning the pieces several times so that they do not stick to the towels. (To store them longer, freeze the ravioli on the baking sheets until firm. Transfer them to a heavy-duty plastic bag, seal tightly, and store in the freezer for up to 1 month. Do not thaw before cooking.)

Bring at least 4 quarts of water to a boil in a large pot. Lower the heat under the pasta pot so that the water boils gently. Add the ravioli and salt to taste. Cook until tender, 2 to 5 minutes depending on the thickness of the ravioli and whether or not they were frozen. Meanwhile, reheat the sauce over low heat. Pour some of the sauce into a heated serving bowl.

Scoop the ravioli out of the pot with a sieve and drain well.

Place the ravioli in the serving bowl. Pour on the remaining sauce. Sprinkle with the cheese and serve immediately.

Calamari Ripieni

Stuffed Calamari

—∿—

Serves 6 to 8
2 1/2 pounds cleaned large calamari (squid)
2 tablespoons olive oil
1 garlic clove, minced
1/2 cup plain bread crumbs
2 tablespoons chopped fresh flat-leaf parsley
2 tablespoons chopped Gaeta olives
2 tablespoons chopped rinsed capers
1/2 teaspoon dried oregano
Salt and freshly ground pepper

For the Sauce
1/4 cup olive oil
1 large garlic clove, lightly crushed
1/2 cup dry red wine
2 cups chopped Italian peeled tomatoes, with their juices
Pinch of crushed red pepper
Salt

——————— ✿ ✿ ✿ ———————

Wash the calamari under cool running water. Set the bodies aside. Chop the tentacles with a large knife or in a food processor.

In a medium skillet, combine oil and garlic and cook over medium heat for 1 minute, or until the garlic begins to turn golden. Stir in the chopped tentacles and cook, stirring, for 2 minutes. Add the bread crumbs, parsley, olives, capers, and oregano. Add salt and pepper to taste. Let cool.

With a small spoon, stuff the bread crumb mixture into the calamari bodies. Do not fill them more than half-full. Pin the calamari closed with wooden toothpicks.

To make the sauce, choose a skillet large enough to hold all of the calamari in a single layer. Pour in the oil and add the garlic. Cook over medium heat for 1 minute until just golden. Add the calamari and cook, turning them gently, until they are just opaque, about 2 minutes on each side.

Add the wine and bring to a simmer. Stir in the tomatoes, crushed red pepper, and salt to taste. Bring to a simmer. Partially cover the pan and cook for 50 to 60 minutes, turning the calamari occasionally, until they are very tender. Add a little water if the sauce becomes too thick.

Serve hot.

Osso Buco a la Bucco

—◊—

Serves 4

1/4 cup all-purpose flour
4 meaty slices veal shank, about 1 1/2 inches thick
2 tablespoons unsalted butter
1 tablespoon olive oil
Salt and freshly ground pepper
1 small onion, finely chopped
1/2 cup dry white wine
1 cup peeled, seeded, and chopped fresh tomatoes or chopped canned
   Italian peeled tomatoes
1 cup chicken broth or meat broth
2 garlic cloves, finely chopped
2 tablespoons minced fresh flat-leaf parsley
1 teaspoon grated lemon zest

———————— ❖ ❖ ❖ ————————

Spread the flour on a piece of wax paper. Dredge the veal in the flour, shaking off the excess.

In a Dutch oven with a tight-fitting lid, melt the butter with the oil over medium heat. Add the veal and sprinkle it with salt and pepper. Cook until browned. Turn the slices and sprinkle with salt and pepper. Scatter the onion around the meat. Cook until the onion is tender, about 10 minutes.

Add the wine and cook, scraping the bottom of the pan with a wooden spoon. Stir in the tomatoes and broth and bring to a simmer. Partially cover the pan and cook, basting the meat occasionally with the sauce, for 1 1/2 hours or until the veal is tender and coming away from the bone. If there is too much liquid, remove the cover and allow some of the liquid to evaporate.

Meanwhile, about 5 minutes before serving, chop together the garlic, parsley, and lemon zest.

Stir the lemon zest mixture into the sauce in the pan and baste the meat. Serve immediately.

Quail Sinatra-Style

—m—

Serves 4 to 6

8 fresh or thawed frozen quail
8 ounces Italian-style fennel pork sausages
2 tablespoons very finely chopped sun-dried tomatoes
1 cup dry white wine
1 tablespoon chopped fresh rosemary
1 garlic clove, minced
Salt and freshly ground pepper
Chopped fresh flat-leaf parsley

——————— ✿ ✿ ✿ ———————

Preheat the oven to 375°F.

Rinse the quail and pat them dry. Tuck the wing tips under the backs.

Remove the sausage meat from the casing. Mix the sausage meat with the sun-dried tomatoes. Put some meat mixture inside each quail. With kitchen twine, tie the legs together.

Put the quail in a covered flameproof casserole large enough to hold them in a single layer. Add the wine, rosemary, garlic, and salt and pepper to taste. Cover and bake for 1 hour.

Uncover and cook, basting two or three times, for 30 to 40 minutes longer, or until the quail is very tender and browned. Transfer the quail to a serving platter. Cover and keep warm.

Place the casserole on top of the stove and bring the liquid to a simmer over medium heat. Cook until thickened and reduced to a glaze. Spoon the sauce over the quail. Sprinkle with parsley and serve immediately.

Chicken Scarpariello

—✿✿—

Serves 6

1 pound Italian-style pork sausages
1/4 cup olive oil
1 chicken (about 3 pounds), cut into 18 pieces
Salt and freshly ground pepper
6 large garlic cloves, thinly sliced
1/4 cup chicken broth
1 cup pickled sweet peppers, cut into bite-sized pieces
1/4 cup white wine vinegar or pickling liquid from the peppers

——————— ✿ ✿ ✿ ———————

Place the sausages in a medium skillet and prick them all over with a fork. Add cold water to come halfway up the sausages. Cover the pan, place over medium heat, and cook until the water has evaporated and the sausages are cooked through. Uncover and cook until browned all over. Cut the sausages into 1-inch pieces.

In a skillet large enough to hold all of the chicken in a single layer, heat the oil over medium heat. Pat the chicken pieces dry and place them in the pan. Sprinkle with salt and pepper. Cook, stirring occasionally, until golden, about 10 minutes. Add the garlic and cook for 2 to 3 minutes more.

Tip the pan and spoon off most of the fat. Add the sausages, broth, peppers, and vinegar. Turn the heat to high and cook, stirring often, for 10 to 15 minutes, or until the liquid is reduced to a light glaze. Serve immediately.

Chicken Francese

—〜—

Serves 4

1 pound thin-sliced chicken cutlets
Salt and freshly ground pepper
2 large eggs
1/2 cup all-purpose flour
1/2 cup chicken broth
1/4 cup dry white wine
2 to 3 tablespoons fresh lemon juice (to taste)
3 tablespoons olive oil
3 tablespoons unsalted butter
1 tablespoon chopped fresh flat-leaf parsley
Lemon wedges

————————　❖ ❖ ❖　————————

Place the chicken cutlets between two sheets of plastic wrap. With a meat pounder or mallet, gently pound the slices to about a 1/4-inch thickness. Sprinkle the chicken generously with salt and pepper.

Put the eggs in a shallow bowl, season with salt and pepper, and beat until well blended. Spread the flour on a plate. Mix together the broth, wine, and lemon juice in a measuring cup or bowl.

Heat the oil with the butter in a large skillet over medium heat until sizzling. Dip only enough of the cutlets in the flour as will fit in the pan in a single layer, dip them in the egg, and add to the pan. Cook for 2 to 3 minutes per side, or until golden brown. Regulate the heat so that the butter does not burn. Transfer the chicken to a plate and keep it warm. Repeat with the remaining chicken.

When all of the chicken is done, add the broth mixture to the pan. Raise the heat and cook, scraping the bottom of the pan, until the sauce is slightly thickened. Stir in the parsley.

Return the chicken pieces to the skillet and turn them once or twice in the sauce. Serve immediately, with lemon wedges.

Pasta all'Amatriciana

Bucatini Amatrice-style

—ɱ—

Serves 4 to 6

2 tablespoons olive oil
2 ounces thick-sliced pancetta, cut into small dice
1 medium onion, finely chopped
1 garlic clove, finely chopped
One 28- to 35-ounce can Italian peeled tomatoes, drained and chopped
Pinch of crushed red pepper
Salt
1 pound bucatini or perciatelli (pasta)
1/2 cup freshly grated Pecorino Romano

✿ ✿ ✿

In a skillet or saucepan large enough to hold the cooked pasta, combine the oil, pancetta, onion, and garlic. Cook, stirring occasionally, over medium heat until the pancetta and onion are golden, about 12 minutes.

Stir in the tomatoes and crushed red pepper. Add salt to taste. Bring to a simmer and cook, stirring occasionally, until the sauce is thickened, about 25 minutes.

Meanwhile, bring at least 4 quarts of water to a boil in a large pot. Add the bucatini and salt to taste, immediately stir the pasta, and cook, stirring occasionally, until the pasta is al dente, tender yet firm to the bite.

Scoop out about 1 cup of the cooking water. Drain the pasta and pour it into the pan with the sauce. Toss the pasta and sauce together over high heat for about 1 minute, until the pasta is coated. Add a little cooking water if the pasta seems dry. Remove from the heat, add the cheese, and toss well. Serve immediately.

Fiori di Zucca Fritti

Fried Zucchini Flowers

Serves 4

1/3 cup all-purpose flour
1/3 cup cornstarch
Salt and freshly ground pepper
1/2 cup sparkling mineral water
Vegetable oil for deep-frying
16 zucchini or other squash blossoms

❖ ❖ ❖

In a small bowl, whisk together the flour, cornstarch, 1/2 teaspoon salt, and pepper to taste. Stir in the water. Let stand for 1 hour.

Pour 2 inches of oil into a deep fryer or deep heavy saucepan. Heat over medium heat until the temperature reaches 375°F on a deep-frying thermometer, or a drop of the batter sizzles and quickly rises to the surface of the oil.

Dip a zucchini flower in the batter, coating it completely. Slip into the oil. Dip and add only as many more flowers as fit without crowding the pan. Fry, turning once, for 1 to 2 minutes, until crisp. Remove the flowers from the pan with a slotted spoon, and drain on paper towels. Fry the remainder, and serve immediately.

Veal Piccata with Capers

—m—

Serves 4

1 pound veal cutlets
Salt and freshly ground pepper
1/4 cup all-purpose flour
2 tablespoons unsalted butter
1 tablespoon olive oil
1/2 cup chicken broth
2 tablespoons rinsed and chopped capers
1 tablespoon fresh lemon juice
1 tablespoon chopped fresh flat-leaf parsley

❖ ❖ ❖

Place the veal cutlets between two sheets of plastic wrap. With a meat pounder or mallet, pound to a 1/4-inch thickness. Sprinkle the meat with salt and pepper.

Spread the flour on a plate. Dredge the cutlets in the flour and shake off the excess. Coat only enough cutlets that will fit in the pan at one time without crowding.

Melt 1 tablespoon of the butter with the oil in a large skillet over medium heat. Add to the pan and brown the cutlets on both sides. Transfer them to a plate. Keep warm. Repeat with the remaining veal.

When all of the cutlets are browned, pour the chicken broth into the pan. Cook over high heat, scraping the bottom of the pan, until the liquid is slightly thickened. Stir in the capers, lemon juice, and parsley. Remove from the heat and swirl in the remaining 1 tablespoon butter.

Pour the sauce over the veal and serve immediately.

CHARMAINE AND ARTIE BUCCO

CHAPTER SIX

Cooking for the Whole Famiglia

PARTY PLANNING WITH CHARMAINE BUCCO

harmaine is my wife and the mother of our children. We've had our differences over the years but remain steadfast on two issues—the greater good of our offspring and maintaining the highest standards of excellence at our restaurant. Charmaine has been my 50/50 business partner in Bucco's Vesuvio and Nuovo Vesuvio since the day my father handed me the chef's toque. Our partnership has survived inflated cheese prices, two Italian wine embargoes, multiple recessions, and a devastating fire.❈

Our family restaurants have enjoyed success over the years partly because Artie and I have both stuck to our strong suits—he's the Toscanini of *la cucina,* and with an AA degree in accounting, I run the business. At first "the business" was buying enough pork cutlets to feed the weekend crowd, but as word spread, so did our culinary obligations to the community. In 1993,

we started Vesuvio Catering. Since then, I have never worked harder nor gained such deep satisfaction in "feeding the masses."

When Italian-Americans gather—for a baptism, the confirmation of a budding teen, or just the need to feel the refuge of the clan—food is the common denominator, the binder, the glue of tradition, blood ties, and good health. There are many options today for feeding a party of forty—yard-long sub sandwiches, gallon jars of Chinese chicken salad, or, for the bigger budgets, a sushi chef who makes house calls. But none of these will cut it at a multigenerational Italian affair.

"Big" doesn't have to mean "bad." Most Old World Italian dishes were made for "big" in the first place—a big farm family with a dozen kids, three generations of elders, plus shiftless Uncle 'Weegi living in the barn. If you choose to prepare this big meal yourself rather than call in a quality catering service, then please, be my guest—but don't settle for the cocktail wieners and ambrosia that pass for a buffet at Rudy and Judy Mayonnaissers' down the street.

Pizza, an old, old Neapolitan tradition, is a wonderful choice for a feast of many mouths, but make it like pizza should be made—fresh ingredients, a thoughtful blend of tastes and textures, and a fun cooking event that even the kids can join in. The other dishes I offer here probably won't involve kids, unless you have an Artie-in-training, but they are as good in fifty portions as they are in two. Serve them, and your guests won't get tipsy first. They'll eat and rave and rave and eat, then get tipsy. Have plenty of strong coffee, and they'll leave knowing that the envelope full of cash they stuck into your Billy or Melissa's pocket was a small price to pay for such splendid repast—what my grandfather called *una bella mangiata* ("a great meal")—and the priceless bonhomie of friends and family.

THANKSGIVING MENU

ANTIPASTO
Provolone, Roasted Peppers, Vinegar Peppers,
Tunafish, Olives, etc.

ZUPPA
Meatballs And Escarole

PASTA
Baked Manicott'

SECONDO
Roast Turkey
(stuffed with Italian Sausage, Peppers, Onions, etc.)
Steamed Broccoli with lemon & olive oil
Fried Mushrooms

FRUTTI
Apples, Pears, Grapes, Fresh Fennel

DOLCI
Cannoli, Pasticiotti, Sflogliatelle

Party Tips by Carmela and Charmaine

I sat down with my longtime friend, Carmela Soprano, to discuss the perfect party from both my view, that of the professional caterer, and her view, that of the seasoned hostess. Here are some collective tips.

CARMELA: Begin planning weeks, if not months, in advance. Of course, if someone drops dead, that's hard to do. The solution: the "Drop Dead" Emergency Party Plan. You know it's coming, why not plan for it?

CHARMAINE: If you are on a tight budget, splurge on appetizers (antipasto) and desserts (dolci) and cut corners on the main course. Or just eliminate the main course altogether. Only the real moochers will notice. Try not to invite them.

CARMELA: Just one person with a sour disposition can ruin the most carefully planned family get-together. If they must come, quarantine them as best you can. Sit them next to a boring person or have them study the rules of a new board game.

CHARMAINE: If you do choose to bring in professional caterers, treat them like members of the family. No one likes a bossy, holier-than-thou hostess. Introduce the caterers to the guests and let them shine. After all, without them, you'd be serving Ritz crackers and Monterey Jack and dashing to the kitchen every two minutes for more bridge mix.

CARMELA: Very important: if you plan to drink to excess, wait until after your guests have gone home. Sure, sip a little wine to loosen up, but watch it. A person having too good a time at their own fund-raiser can go from pleasant to pathetic in a heartbeat and engender damaging gossip. Trust me, I've seen it happen!

CHARMAINE: Halfway through the party, be sure to offer a toast to the caterer. If you did the work yourself, speak to a good friend beforehand about this. It's not just food, after all. When your guests remember this affair, their taste buds will speak first, and you want those buds to whisper your name with admiration and respect.

CARMELA: For all but family affairs, have a going-away gift for guests. Make sure it's something unique that can be bought in bulk. Little porcelain angels are always a hit.

CHARMAINE: It is absolutely de rigueur to tip the caterer. This is no place to cut corners.

Pollo Cacciatore al Forno

Baked Chicken Cacciatore

—m—

For 4	For 50
One 3-pound chicken, cut into 8 pieces	13 chickens
Salt and freshly ground pepper	
2 tablespoons olive oil	About 1 cup
2 green bell peppers, cured, seeded, and cut into narrow strips	26
1 large onion, thinly sliced	13
8 ounces mushrooms, trimmed and quartered	6 pounds
2 garlic cloves, finely chopped	12
2 cups canned Italian peeled tomatoes, drained and chopped	Six 28-ounce cans
1 teaspoon dried oregano	1/4 cup

——————— ✿ ✿ ✿ ———————

Preheat the oven to 450°F. Oil one or more roasting pans, to hold the chicken pieces in a single layer.

Rinse the chicken and pat dry. Arrange the pieces skin side down in the pan(s). Sprinkle with salt and pepper. Bake the chicken for 30 minutes.

Turn the chicken pieces and sprinkle the skin side with salt and pepper. Bake for 20 minutes more, or until lightly browned.

While the chicken cooks, in one or more large skillets, heat the oil over medium heat. Add the peppers, onions, and mushrooms in a shallow layer. Cook, stirring frequently, until the vegetables are tender and lightly browned, about 15 minutes.

Stir in the garlic and cook for 2 minutes. Add the tomatoes, oregano, and salt and pepper to taste. Bring to a simmer and cook until the sauce is thick, about 30 minutes.

Spoon off some of the fat from around the chicken. Pour the sauce and vegetables over and around the pieces. Bake 20 minutes longer. Serve hot.

Ah Beetz'

Pizza

—∾—

For 1 pizza, serving 8 to 10
1 envelope active dry yeast
1 1/3 cups warm water (105° to 115°F)
3 1/2 to 4 cups all-purpose flour
2 teaspoons salt

For the Sauce
2 pounds fresh plum tomatoes, peeled,
  seeded, and chopped, or one 28-ounce can
  Italian crushed tomatoes
1 garlic clove, finely chopped
1/4 cup olive oil
Salt
4 fresh basil leaves, torn into bits

For the Topping:
12 ounces fresh mozzarella, thinly sliced
1/2 cup freshly grated Pecorino Romano
  or Parmigiano-Reggiano
Olive oil

For 6 pizzas, serving 50
6 envelopes
8 cups
21 to 24 cups
1/4 cup

12 pounds fresh or 6 cans

6 garlic cloves
1 1/2 cups

24

4 1/2 pounds
3 cups

———— ✿ ✿ ✿ ————

For each pizza, sprinkle the yeast over the water in a small bowl. Let stand for 1 minute, or until the yeast is creamy. Stir until the yeast dissolves.

In a large bowl, combine 3 1/2 cups of the flour and the salt. Add the yeast mixture and stir until a soft dough forms. Turn the dough out onto a lightly floured surface and knead, adding more flour if necessary, until smooth and elastic, about 10 minutes.

Lightly coat a large bowl with oil. Place the dough in the bowl, turning it to oil the top. Cover with plastic wrap. Place in a warm, draft-free place and let rise until doubled, about 1 1/2 hours.

Oil a 15 x 10 x 1-inch jelly-roll pan. With your fist, flatten the dough. Place the dough in the center of the pan and stretch and flatten it out to fit. Cover it with plastic wrap and let it rise for about 1 hour, until puffy and nearly doubled in bulk.

To make the sauce, in a large saucepan, combine the tomatoes, garlic, oil, and salt to taste. Bring to a simmer and cook, stirring occasionally, until thickened, 15 to 20 minutes. Add the basil. Let the sauce cool.

Preheat the oven to 450°F.

With your fingertips, firmly press the dough to make dimples at 1-inch intervals all over the surface. Spread the sauce over the dough, leaving a 1/2-inch border all around. Bake for 20 minutes.

Remove the pizza from the oven. Arrange the slices of cheese on top. Sprinkle with the grated cheese. Drizzle with oil. Return the pizza to the oven and bake for 5 minutes, or until the cheese is melted and the crust is browned. Cut into squares and serve hot.

Sfinciuni

Sicilian Onion Pizza

—✍—

For 1 Pizza, Serving 10	For 5 Pizzas, Serving 50
1 envelope active dry yeast	5 envelopes
1 cup warm water (105° to 115°F)	5 cups
2 tablespoons olive oil	10 tablespoons
3 to 3 1/2 cups unbleached all-purpose flour	15 to 17 1/2 cups
1 teaspoon salt	5 teaspoons
1/4 teaspoon freshly ground pepper	1 1/4 teaspoons

For the Topping:

1 large onion, thinly sliced	5
1/4 cup olive oil	1 1/4 cups
2 cups peeled, chopped canned Italian tomatoes	10 cups (about three 28-ounce cans)
1 teaspoon dried oregano	5 teaspoons
Salt and freshly ground pepper	
8 anchovy fillets or 1 can (2 ounces) anchovy fillets, drained and chopped	40 anchovy fillets or 5 cans
1/2 cup plain bread crumbs	2 1/2 cups
1/2 cup provolone cut into 1/2-inch cubes	2 1/2 cups

———— ✿ ✿ ✿ ————

For each pizza, sprinkle the yeast over the water in a small bowl. Let stand for 1 minute, or until creamy. Stir until the yeast dissolves.

In a large bowl, combine 3 cups of the flour, the salt, and pepper. Add the yeast mixture and the oil and stir until a soft dough forms. Turn the dough out onto a lightly floured surface and knead until smooth and elastic, adding more flour as necessary if the dough is sticky.

Oil a large bowl. Place the dough in the bowl, turning it once to oil the top. Cover with a towel and let rise in a warm draft-free place until doubled, about one hour.

To make the topping, cook the onion in 2 tablespoons of the oil in a medium saucepan until tender and golden, about 7 minutes. Add the tomatoes, oregano, and pepper and salt to taste. Cook for 15 to 20 minutes, until the sauce is slightly thickened. Stir in the anchovies, remove from the heat, and let cool.

In a small skillet, heat 1 tablespoon of the oil. Add the bread crumbs and cook over medium heat until toasted and browned.

Oil a 12-inch round pizza pan. Place the dough in the pan and stretch and pat it out evenly to fit the pan. Cover and let rise for 30 minutes, or until almost doubled.

Preheat the oven to 425°F.

Press your fingertips into the dough at 1-inch intervals to form dimples. Spread half of the sauce on the dough, leaving a 1/2-inch border all around. Bake for 25 minutes.

Spread the remaining sauce on the dough. Scatter the cheese on top and sprinkle with the bread crumbs. Drizzle with the remaining 2 tablespoons oil. Bake 5 to 10 minutes more, until the cheese is melted and the pizza is browned around the edges. Cut the pizza into wedges and serve immediately.

Roasted Sausages, Peppers, Potatoes, and Onions

—m—

For 4	For 50
1 pound potatoes, peeled and cut into 1-inch chunks	12 pounds
1 green bell pepper, cored, seeded, and cut into 1-inch pieces	15
1 red bell pepper, cored, seeded, and cut into 1-inch pieces	15
1 medium onion, cut into 1-inch chunks	12
1/4 cup olive oil	2 1/2 cups
Salt and freshly ground pepper	
1 pound Italian-style pork sausages	15 pounds

——————— ✿ ✿ ✿ ———————

Preheat the oven to 450°F.

Spread the vegetables in a single layer in one or more large shallow roasting pans; do not crowd them, or they will not brown. Drizzle with the oil and sprinkle with salt and pepper to taste. Stir well.

Roast the vegetables, stirring once or twice, for 45 minutes.

Pierce each sausage in two or three places with a fork. Place the sausages on top of the vegetables. Bake for 15 to 30 minutes, or until the sausages and vegetables are cooked through. Serve hot.

Eggplant Parmigiana

—〰—

For 6	For 50
2 medium eggplants (about 1 pound)	15
Salt	
Olive oil or vegetable oil for pan frying	
2 1/2 cups Marinara Sauce (page 13)	6 quarts
8 ounces fresh mozzarella, thinly sliced	5 pounds
1/2 cup freshly grated Pecorino Romano or Parmigiano-Reggiano	5 cups

✿ ✿ ✿

Trim the eggplants and cut them into 1/4-inch-thick slices. Layer the slices in one or more colanders, sprinkling each layer with salt. Let drain for 30 minutes.

Rinse the eggplant and pat dry. Pour about 1/2 inch oil into one or more large deep skillets and heat over medium heat. Fry the slices, in batches, in a single layer, turning once, until browned on both sides. Drain on paper towels.

Preheat the oven to 350°F.

Spread a thin layer of tomato sauce in one or more shallow baking dishes. Make a layer of eggplant slices, overlapping them slightly. Top with a layer of mozzarella, another layer of sauce, and a sprinkle of grated cheese. Repeat the layering, ending with eggplant, sauce, and grated cheese. (The eggplant can be made ahead to this point with plastic wrap. Cover and refrigerate for several hours, or overnight. Remove it from the refrigerator about 30 minutes before baking.)

Bake for 45 to 60 minutes, or until the sauce is bubbling and the mozzarella is melted. Let stand for 10 minutes before serving.

Caesar Salad

—◊◊—

For 6	For 50
For the Croutons	
6 slices Italian or French bread, cut into (1/2 inch thick) bite-sized cubes	4 to 5 loaves
1/4 cup extra virgin olive oil	2 cups
For the Salad	
1 large egg	8
1 large garlic clove, very finely minced	8
4 anchovy fillets, drained and chopped	5 cans (2 ounces each)
1 tablespoon fresh lemon juice	3/4 cup
1 teaspoon Worcestershire sauce	3 tablespoons
Salt and freshly ground pepper	
1/2 cup freshly grated Parmigiano-Reggiano	4 cups
1/3 cup extra virgin olive oil	3 cups
1 head romaine lettuce (about 1 1/4 pounds), washed, dried, and torn into bite-sized pieces	8

To make the croutons, preheat the oven to 325°F.

Spread the bread cubes in a single layer in one or more large shallow roasting pans. Drizzle with the olive oil and toss well. Bake, stirring occasionally, until the bread is toasted and golden brown, about 20 minutes. Set aside.

To make the salad, place the egg(s) in a saucepan and cover with cold water. Bring the water to a boil over medium heat. Cook for 1 1/2 minutes. Drain the egg(s) and cool under running water. Peel.

In a large bowl, combine the garlic and anchovies. Mash them together into a paste. Beat in the egg(s), lemon juice, Worcestershire, and salt and pepper to taste. Gradually beat in the cheese and olive oil. Taste for seasoning.

Toss the lettuce with the dressing. Sprinkle with the croutons. Toss again and taste for seasoning. Serve immediately.

Insalata di Mare

Seafood Salad

—〰—

For 6	For 50
2 pounds mussels	16 pounds
Salt	
1 pound medium shrimp, shelled and deveined	8 pounds
1 pound cleaned calamari (squid), cut crosswise into 1/2-inch rings	8 pounds
1 cup thinly sliced celery	8 cups
1 cup sliced pitted green olives	8 cups
1/3 cup extra virgin olive oil	2 1/2 cups
1/2 teaspoon grated lemon zest	1 1/2 tablespoons
2 tablespoons fresh lemon juice, or to taste	1 cup, or to taste
2 tablespoons chopped fresh flat-leaf parsley	1 cup
2 garlic cloves, minced	16
Pinch of crushed red pepper	To taste
1 lemon, cut into wedges	6

——————— ✿ ✿ ✿ ———————

Place the mussels in cold water to cover for 30 minutes.

Scrub the mussels with a stiff brush and scrape off any barnacles or seaweed. Discard any mussels with cracked shells or that do not shut tightly when tapped. Remove the beards by pulling them toward the narrow end of the shells.

Place the mussels in a large pot with 1/2 cup water. Cover and cook until the mussels open, 5 to 10 minutes. Discard any that refuse to open.

Bring a large saucepan of water to a simmer. Add salt to taste and the shrimp. Cook for 2 to 3 minutes, until the shrimp are just cooked through. Scoop out the shrimp and cool them under cold running water; drain well. Leave the water boiling in the pot.

Drop the calamari into the boiling water and cook just until opaque, about 1 minute. Drain thoroughly and cool under cold running water.

Cut the shrimp into bite-sized pieces. Combine the shrimp, calamari, mussels, celery, and olives in a large bowl.

Whisk together the oil, lemon zest, lemon juice, parsley, garlic, salt to taste, and the crushed red pepper.

Pour the dressing over the salad mixture and toss well. (If you are making the salad ahead of time, toss with only half the dressing; cover and refrigerate for up to 2 hours. Toss with the remaining dressing just before serving.) Taste for seasoning. Garnish with the lemon wedges.

Almond Torte

—∿—

Serves 8

2 cups blanched almonds
1 cup sugar
2 tablespoons all-purpose flour
1/2 teaspoon baking powder
1/2 teaspoon salt
6 large eggs, at room temperature
1 teaspoon vanilla extract
1/2 teaspoon almond extract
1/2 cup seedless raspberry jam
4 ounces semisweet or bittersweet chocolate
1/2 cup heavy cream

——————— ✿ ✿ ✿ ———————

Preheat the oven to 350°F. Butter two 9-inch layer cake pans. Line the pans with circles of wax paper. Butter the paper and sprinkle the pans with flour. Tap out the excess.

In a food processor or blender, combine the almonds and 1/4 cup of the sugar. Grind the nuts very fine. Blend in the flour, baking powder, and salt.

In the large bowl of an electric mixer, beat the egg yolks until thick and light. Beat in the remaining 3/4 cup sugar and the extracts. Stir in the almond mixture.

In a clean bowl, with clean beaters, whip the egg whites until soft peaks form. Gently fold the whites into the almond mixture with a rubber spatula.

Scrape the batttter into the prepared pans. Bake for 20 to 25 minutes, or until the cake springs back when touched in the center. Cool on a wire rack for 10 minutes. Unmold the cakes and carefully peel off the paper. Turn the cakes right side up and let cool completely.

Place four strips of wax paper around the edges of a cake plate. Place one cake layer upside down on the plate. Spread the jam evenly over the top. Place the second cake layer right side up on the first layer.

Break up the chocolate into small pieces. In a small heatproof bowl set over, not in, a pan of simmering water, melt the chocolate with the heavy cream. Stir until smooth. Let the glaze cool slightly.

Pour the glaze onto the top of the cake. Smooth the top with a metal spatula, allowing some of the chocolate to run down the sides of the cake. Then smooth the chocolate over the sides. Let set briefly, then remove the wax paper strips. Chill briefly to set the chocolate.

DR. JENNIFER MELFI AND DR. RICHARD LA PENNA

CHAPTER SEVEN

Rage, Guilt, Loneliness, and Food

EXCERPTS FROM A PAPER BY DR. JENNIFER MELFI, M.D., M.A., M.F.T., AND DR. RICHARD LA PENNA, M.D.

I came across this research paper while doing my own digging at the Newark Public Library. The authors are both of Italian descent and practicing psychiatrists in the Newark/Essex County area. The question they ask: Why do Italian-Americans care so much about food? Is it a sign of some deep-seated cultural neurosis? In this brief excerpt, the doctors weigh in. ❁

Our interest in Italian-American food rituals comes from our own upbringing and our mutual discomfort at having to eat and eat and eat wherever we went. We assembled a random group of 250 subjects with obviously Italian names from area phone books. We sat each subject down and asked him or her questions about food and self. We then built a statistical model to illuminate common themes and problems. Of course, as with all statistics, there is a margin of error.

Of all the subjects, male and female, 98 percent strongly agreed with the statement, "I like food." But only a surprising 72 percent agreed with the follow-up statement, "I always feel good after eating." Probing deeper, we found that the remaining respondents (28 percent) had lingering feelings of guilt and self-loathing after eating.

"Why do you keep eating if it makes you feel bad?" we asked these "Guilty Eaters." Sixty-two percent said it was a childhood habit that was "hardwired" into their brains. Parental approval always accompanied eating the most food.

"Otherwise, it was, *'What, are you sick?'* or, *"'Is something wrong with my cooking?'"* said one man, the youngest of six.

Another group of Guilty Eaters (GEs) are the ones who eat *because* they feel guilty about something else. Food becomes a way of assuaging their guilt. One subject, a plumber, confessed that he'd been cheating on his wife for decades. What did he do every time he left his girlfriend's condo? He ate an entire mushroom pizza. Thus he both had an excuse for his absence—stopping off at Joey's Pizza— and he diverted his guilt about the affair into a screaming match with his wife over a cold dinner.

Criminals of Italian ethnicity—an egregious cliché—are often depicted in films as being well-dressed fat guys (think Al Capone) who like to sit down to a feast after they rob, steal, or "whack" someone. And they often eat late at night, almost a fourth meal of the day. There are no known criminals in our survey, but we can see how these people might fit the profile of GEs—their animalistic behavior no doubt fosters shame and a churning stomach.

The Guilty Eaters are close kin to the "Angry Eaters" (AEs), i.e., those who use food as an antidote to petty frustrations and perceived slights. Given our social contract, if a woman cuts you off in traffic, you can't smash her face, can you? You can yell, sure, but the anger persists. For many (44 percent), it only dissipates after gorging.

Last Meal
COMMENTS FROM SOPRANO ASSOCIATES

The question is: if you were on death row, what would you order for a last meal? I asked some frequent patrons of Nuovo Vesuvio.—*AB*

SILVIO DANTE: As is common knowledge, most of your death row executions seen on TV come from Texas and Oklahoma, the nation's leaders in the field. Therefore, most last meals are fried chicken, pork rinds, chili fries, an occasional macaroni & cheese. No self-respecting Italian would go to meet his maker on such crap. Me, I'd let my mother prepare the meal. She knows what I like and what I could handle under such trying circumstances.

CHRISTOPHER MOLTISANTI: Honestly, I'd care more about how I looked than what I ate. I thought that Oklahoma City guy went out well—he looked trim and clean-shaven and his jumpsuit fit him nice. I think

overeating would be a mistake many might make. I'd want just enough in there so my stomach didn't start growling at the wrong time—a slice of pizza, a little red wine, and a final toast to all of those I have both loved and hated.

FURIO GIUNTA: I'd order a ton of food—zuppe, pasta, carne—then when you brought it, I'd spit in your face and laugh.

HERMAN "HESH" RABKIN: I would have a meal catered by Petrossian or perhaps Greengrass, the smoked fish king of New York. Then I would surround myself with good friends and not think about what's to transpire. My fate is not in my hands—only those precious final moments. I'd try to enjoy them.

Finally there are the "Single Eaters" (often stigmatized as the "Lonely Eaters"), and their percentage among women is growing. In our atomized society, we don't all end up with big, loving families of our own. Many of us are unattached professional people and we eat alone. For this group, food provides a link, however slight, to the Italian-American family they either left behind or yearn to have. If food for the GE or AE is a bad thing—leading to obesity, diabetes, and a general avoidance of underlying neuroses—food is often a good thing for the Single Eater. Food is hope, a reminder of what might still come in life if you stay close to your roots. Like the sage said, hope comes in many forms.

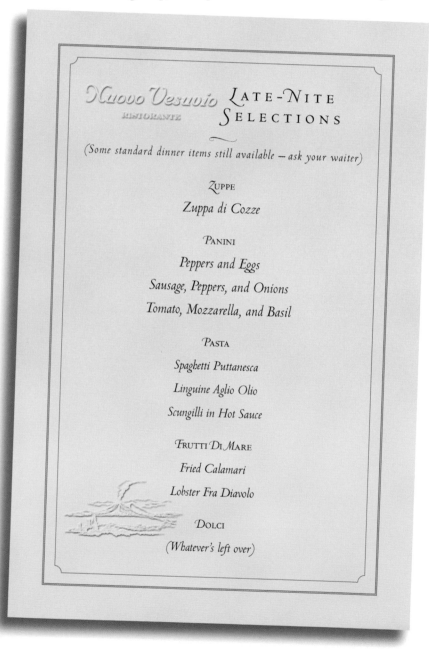

Nuovo Vesuvio RISTORANTE

LATE-NITE SELECTIONS

(Some standard dinner items still available — ask your waiter)

ZUPPE
Zuppa di Cozze

PANINI
Peppers and Eggs

Sausage, Peppers, and Onions

Tomato, Mozzarella, and Basil

PASTA
Spaghetti Puttanesca

Linguine Aglio Olio

Scungilli in Hot Sauce

FRUTTI DI MARE
Fried Calamari

Lobster Fra Diavolo

DOLCI
(Whatever's left over)

Chicken with Parsley Crumbs

—∽—

Serves 4
1 chicken (about 3 pounds), cut up
Salt and freshly ground pepper
1/3 cup plain bread crumbs
2 tablespoons chopped fresh flat-leaf parsley
1 large garlic clove, minced
2 tablespoons Dijon mustard
1 tablespoon olive oil

———— ✿ ✿ ✿ ————

Preheat the oven to 450°F.

Sprinkle the chicken all over with salt and pepper. Place the pieces skin side up in a baking pan. Bake for 30 minutes.

Meanwhile, combine the bread crumbs, parsley, garlic, oil, and salt and pepper to taste in a small bowl.

Brush the chicken with the mustard. Sprinkle with the crumb mixture, patting it on so that it adheres. Bake for 20 to 30 minutes more, or until the juices run clear when the chicken is cut near the bone. Serve hot or cold.

Melfi's Minestrone

—m—

Serves 2

1/4 cup orzo or other small pasta
Salt
One 19-ounce can vegetable soup
1/4 cup chopped ham (about 2 thin slices)
2 tablespoons freshly grated Parmigiano-Reggiano

——————— ❁ ❁ ❁ ———————

Bring a small saucepan of water to a boil. Add the orzo and salt to taste. Cook, stirring occasionally, until the orzo is tender. Drain the pasta, reserving a little of the water.

Meanwhile, heat the soup to a simmer in a medium saucepan.

Stir the ham and cooked orzo into the soup. Add a little of the cooking water if the soup is too thick. Turn off the heat and stir in the cheese. Serve immediately.

Tuna Salad with Green Beans and Tomatoes

Serves 2

One 7-ounce can tuna packed in olive oil
2 medium tomatoes, cut into bite-sized pieces
2 hard-cooked eggs, peeled and quartered
3 or 4 thin slices red onion, quartered
Pinch of dried oregano
1 to 2 tablespoons fresh lemon juice
Salt and freshly ground pepper
8 ounces green beans, cooked, and cut into bite-sized pieces
Lemon wedges

◆ ◆ ◆

Place the tuna, with its oil, in a large bowl. Break it into pieces with a fork.

Add the tomatoes, eggs, and onion. Sprinkle with the oregano, lemon juice, a pinch of salt, and pepper to taste. Toss gently.

Arrange the green beans on a platter. Top with the tuna salad. Garnish with lemon wedges and serve immediately.

Zuppa di Cozze

Mussels in Spicy Tomato Sauce

—✳✳—

Serves 4

4 pounds mussels (or substitute small clams)

4 garlic cloves, very finely chopped, plus 1 whole garlic clove

2 tablespoons chopped fresh flat-leaf parsley

1 small peperoncino, crumbled, or a pinch of crushed red pepper

1/3 cup olive oil

1 cup dry white wine

3 pounds ripe tomatoes, peeled, seeded, and chopped, or two 28- to 35-
ounce cans Italian peeled tomatoes, drained and chopped

Pinch of salt

8 slices Italian bread, toasted

———— ✿ ✿ ✿ ————

Place the mussels in cold water to cover for 30 minutes. Drain and scrub them with a stiff brush. Scrape off any barnacles or seaweed. Discard any mussels with cracked shells or that do not shut tightly when tapped. Remove the beards by pulling them toward the narrow end of the shells.

In a large saucepan, cook the chopped garlic, parsley, and peperoncino in the oil over low heat until the garlic is golden, about 1 minute. Stir in the wine and bring to a simmer. Add the tomatoes and salt. Cook over medium heat, stirring occasionally, until the sauce is slightly thickened, about 20 minutes.

Gently stir in the mussels. Cover the pot. Cook until the mussels open, 5 to 10 minutes. Discard any that refuse to open.

Rub the toast with the garlic clove. Serve with the mussels.

Orange and Fennel Salad

—✿—

Serves 4

2 large navel oranges, peeled and cut crosswise into slices
1 medium fennel bulb, trimmed and very thinly sliced
1/2 red onion, very thinly sliced
12 black olives
3 tablespoons extra virgin olive oil
Salt

——————— ✿ ✿ ✿ ———————

Arrange the orange slices and fennel slices alternately on a platter. Scatter the onion and black olives over the top. Drizzle with the olive oil, sprinkle with salt, and serve.

Arugula and Parmesan Salad

Serves 2

1 bunch arugula, washed and dried
2 tablespoons extra virgin olive oil
2 teaspoons balsamic vinegar
Salt and freshly ground pepper
A small piece of Parmigiano-Reggiano

✿ ✿ ✿

Cut off the arugula stems. Tear the leaves into bite-sized pieces.

In a large bowl, whisk together the oil, vinegar, and salt and pepper to taste. Add the arugula and toss well. Pile the salad onto two plates.

With a vegetable peeler, shave the cheese over the salad. Serve immediately.

Salmon Steaks with Avocado Salsa

—ᴡ—

Serves 2

1 cup plain low-fat yogurt
1 green onion, finely chopped
1 tablespoon chopped fresh basil
Salt
1/2 cup diced ripe avocado
1/2 cup diced seeded tomato
1/2 cup diced seeded cucumber
2 salmon steaks (about 8 ounces each)
1 teaspoon olive oil
Freshly ground pepper

——————— ✿ ✿ ✿ ———————

In a small bowl, stir together the yogurt, green onion, basil, and salt to taste. Fold in the avocado, tomato, and cucumber.

Preheat the broiler. Place the broiler pan about 4 inches from the heat.

Rub the salmon with the oil and sprinkle with salt and pepper. Broil for 4 minutes, or until lightly browned. Turn and cook for 3 to 5 minutes longer, or until slightly translucent when cut near the bone.

Serve the salmon steaks immediately, accompanied by the salsa.

Scungilli in Hot Sauce

—᙭᙭—

Serves 6 to 8

2 pounds partially cooked fresh or frozen scungilli (conch or whelk meat)
1/3 cup olive oil
2 large garlic cloves, finely chopped
Pinch of crushed red pepper, or to taste
3 pounds ripe tomatoes, peeled, seeded, and chopped, or two 28-ounce cans
   Italian peeled tomatoes, chopped, with their juice
1 cup dry white wine
Salt
Friselle (black pepper biscuits) or toasted sliced Italian bread

──────── ✿ ✿ ✿ ────────

If the scungilli are frozen, place them in a bowl with cold water to cover and put the bowl in the refrigerator to thaw, several hours or overnight; change the water occasionally.

Rinse the scungilli. Begin cutting it into 1/4-inch slices; when you come to a dark tube filled with spongy matter, pull or cut it out and discard, as it can be gritty. The tube on the outside of the body does not need to be removed. Rinse the slices well and pat dry.

In a large saucepan, heat the oil with the garlic and crushed red pepper over medium-low heat until the garlic is golden. Add the tomatoes, wine, and salt to taste. Bring to a simmer, reduce the heat to low, and cook for 15 minutes, stirring occasionally.

Add the scungilli and bring to a simmer. Cook, stirring occasionally, for 30 minutes or until the scungilli is tender and the sauce has thickened. If the sauce becomes too thick, stir in a little water. Taste for seasoning.

Meanwhile, if using friselle, sprinkle them with cool water. Let stand for 10 minutes to soften slightly. Break them into chunks.

Place a few pieces of friselle or slices of toasted bread in each of four pasta bowls. Spoon on the scungilli and serve immediately.

Spaghetti Puttanesca

—✳✳✳—

Serves 4 to 6

3 garlic cloves, finely chopped

1 small peperoncino, crumbled, or a pinch of crushed red pepper

1/3 cup olive oil

2 1/2 pounds ripe plum tomatoes, peeled, seeded, and chopped, or one 28-
    to 35-ounce can Italian peeled tomatoes, drained and chopped

1 teaspoon dried oregano

Salt

1/2 cup pitted and chopped oil-cured olives

1/4 cup capers, rinsed

8 to 12 anchovy fillets, drained

1/4 cup finely chopped fresh flat-leaf parsley

1 pound spaghetti

————————— ✿ ✿ ✿ —————————

In a skillet large enough to hold the sauce and the cooked pasta, cook the garlic and the peperoncino in the olive oil over low heat until the garlic is golden. Raise the heat to medium and add the tomatoes, oregano, and a pinch of salt. Cook for 15 to 20 minutes, or until the sauce is thickened.

Stir in the olives, capers, anchovies, and parsley and cook 2 minutes more.

Meanwhile, bring at least 4 quarts of water to a boil in a large pot. Add salt to taste and the spaghetti. Cook, stirring frequently, until the pasta is al dente, tender yet still firm to the bite. Drain the pasta and add it to the simmering sauce.

Toss well. Serve immediately.

Linguine Aglio Olio

Linguine with Garlic and Oil

—◍—

Serves 4

1/3 cup fruity olive oil
2 to 3 tablespoons minced garlic
1 small peperoncino, crumbled, or 1/2 teaspoon crushed red pepper
1/3 cup chopped fresh flat-leaf parsley
1 pound linguine
Salt

———— ✿ ✿ ✿ ————

Pour the olive oil into a large skillet. Add the garlic and peperoncino and cook, stirring, over medium-low heat for 3 minutes, or until the garlic is lightly golden. Stir in the parsley and turn off the heat.

Meanwhile, bring at least 4 quarts of water to a boil in a large pot. Add the pasta and salt to taste. Cook, stirring frequently, until the pasta is al dente, tender yet still firm to the bite.

Set aside a cup of the cooking water. Drain the pasta and add it to the skillet with the sauce. Cook over medium heat, tossing until the pasta is well coated with the sauce. Add a little of the reserved cooking water if the pasta seems dry. Serve immediately.

Calamari Fritti

Fried Calamari

—◊◊◊—

Serves 6 to 8

2 pounds cleaned calamari (squid)
1 cup all-purpose flour
1 teaspoon salt
Freshly ground pepper
Olive oil or vegetable oil for deep-frying
Lemon wedges

———— ✿ ✿ ✿ ————

Rinse the calamari thoroughly inside and out. Drain well. Cut the bodies crosswise into 1/2-inch rings. Cut the tentacles in half through the base. Pat dry.

Spread the flour on a sheet of wax paper and season with the salt and pepper to taste.

Pour 2 inches of oil into a deep heavy saucepan or a deep fryer. Heat the oil to 375°F on a deep-frying thermometer, or until a small piece of the calamari sizzles and rises to the surface when added to the oil. When the temperature is reached, lightly roll a few pieces of calamari in the flour mixture. Shake off the excess flour. Slip the pieces into the hot oil, without crowding the pan, and cook until the calamari are a light golden brown, about 3 minutes. With a slotted spoon, transfer the calamari to paper towels to drain. Repeat with the remaining calamari.

Serve hot with lemon wedges.

Lobster Fra Diavolo

Lobster in Spicy Tomato Sauce with Linguine

—◊—

Serves 4 to 6

2 live lobsters (about 1 1/2 pounds each)
2 large garlic cloves, lightly crushed
1 small dried peperoncino, crumbled, or a pinch of crushed red pepper
1/3 cup olive oil
1 cup dry white wine
One 28- to 35-ounce can Italian peeled tomatoes, chopped or passed
    through a food mill
2 tablespoons chopped fresh flat-leaf parsley
1/2 teaspoon dried oregano
Salt
1 pound linguine or spaghetti

——————— ✿ ✿ ✿ ———————

Place the lobsters upside down on a cutting board. Do not remove the rubber bands that keep the lobster claws shut. To kill the lobsters, protecting your hand with a heavy towel or pot holder, hold each lobster above the tail and plunge the point of a heavy chef's knife into the body where the tail joins the chest, and cut off the tails. Cut the lobsters at the joints into 1- to 2-inch chunks. Crack the claws.

In a large heavy saucepan, cook the lobster pieces, garlic, and peperoncino in the oil over medium-low heat, stirring often, for 10 minutes. Add the wine and cook for 1 minute. Add the tomatoes, parsley, oregano, and salt to taste. Bring to a simmer. Cook, stirring occasionally, until the sauce is thickened, about 30 minutes. Remove the lobster pieces and keep them warm.

Meanwhile, bring at least 4 quarts of water to a boil in a large pot. Add salt to taste and the linguine and stir well. Cook, stirring frequently, until the linguine is al dente, tender yet still firm to the bite. Drain.

Toss the linguine with the sauce. Arrange the linguine in a warm shallow serving bowl and top with the lobster. Serve immediately.

Pears al Vino Bianco

—〜—

Serves 6
6 Bosc or Anjou pears (not too ripe)
1 1/2 cups dry white wine
1/2 cup water
3/4 cup sugar
2 strips lemon zest, about 2 inches long
1 vanilla bean

❂ ❂ ❂

With a demitasse spoon or melon baller, working from the bottom of the pears, scoop out the core and seeds.

In a saucepan large enough to hold all of the pears upright, bring the wine, water, sugar, lemon zest, and vanilla bean to a simmer over medium heat, stirring until the sugar is dissolved. Add the pears and reduce the heat to low. Cover the pan and cook, turning the pears once, for 20 minutes, or until they are tender throughout when pierced with a small knife.

Transfer the pears to a serving dish. Turn the heat under the pan to medium-high and cook the syrup until thickened and golden, about 10 minutes.

Pour the syrup over the pears. Let cool slightly, then cover and chill before serving.

PETER PAUL "PAULIE WALNUTS" GUALTIERI AND NUCCI

CHAPTER EIGHT

My Nucci

BY PETER PAUL "PAULIE WALNUTS" GUALTIERI

Peter Gualtieri, known to all as "Paulie Walnuts," is a good friend and a man who exemplifies perhaps the highest of all Italian-American virtues— the love for one's mother. Here, in his own words, he speaks of his mother, "Nucci" Gualtieri, at that time living in Nutley, New Jersey, and how she taught him the glory and solace of food. She has since relocated to the Green Grove Retirement Community in West Orange.

My mother is the most important person in my life, bar none. Being without wife and children, at least currently, I have no other family I give a shit about other than my mother. Her name is Nucci (from Marianuccia, or Little Marian) and though she has lived a hard life, full of heartache and tragedy, she has always stood tall. I call her "the Queen."

My father, Gennaro Gualtieri, was a proud man and taught me much about my Italian-American heritage and its struggles. But, tragically, he died when I was only eleven, run over by a trolley. He had spent a good portion of my youth incarcerated for various minor beefs and thus did not leave my mother and us kids much to live on. I feared we would become destitute and have to apply for welfare, like many other minorities. But Nucci, God love her, had other plans.

She made sure I got to school each morning, then went off to work at the Tung-sol light bulb factory. All day she'd weed out defective filaments on the assembly line, and every night she'd make it home in time to fix us a delicious home-cooked meal. I was not a perfect child by any means—I did poorly in school, given an undiagnosed learning disability, and I had a bad habit of conversing with my fists. But in my mother's eyes, I could do no wrong. My brothers and sisters we won't even talk about here, but never have there been better times in my life than, in her later years, just the two of us, Nucci and Paulie, sitting down to an evening meal of pork chops with peppers and garlic and laughing about the day's events.

Cooking and Cleanliness
RULES FOR SANITARY COOKING AND EATING

They say that cleanliness is next to godliness. It is also elbow to elbow with healthiness and therefore a responsibility of each and all. A few common-sense food-related tips.

- *Never walk into a restaurant that doesn't have a health rating of A proudly displayed on its door. A rating of B, C, or D is the same as having rats over for drinks.*

- *Always wash your hands before and after eating, before and after toiletry duties, before and after shaking hands with strangers, and before and after visiting a hospital. Germ-wise, hospitals are where people get sick.*

- *Disinfect and/or bleach kitchen towels, sponges, and cooking utensils on a daily basis. Yesterday's raw chicken is tomorrow's bacterium nightmare.*

- *Always wash your hands after tying or untying your shoes. Shoelaces can come in contact with biohazards on restroom floors. Not a pleasant thought, especially for a cookbook, but nonetheless true, unfortunately.*

- *At a winter event where there are school-age children, wear a face mask and refuse to take even a cookie from one of the kids. I've paid dearly for this one at my sister's house.*

- *Eat all leftovers within 24 hours. That gabagool that's been sitting in there for a week is a trip to the ER, and remember, ERs are where germs meet and mingle.*

Ma is getting on in years and balance problems prohibit her from cooking like she used to. So now, as much as possible, I do the cooking. I take her grocery shopping every Saturday and she picks out the meats and vegetables and bickers about the prices, just like always. I then fix the big meal of the day, along with a few dishes she can keep in the refrigerator and warm up during the week. I also take her to her weekly hairdressing

COOKING FOR THE BOYS
I like to cook for my friends and associates at work. On a cold day down at the shop, I'll cook up a nice beans & 'shcarole soup and warm our collective cockles, so to speak. Or maybe a potatoes & eggs sandwich. It improves morale.

"Why Do They Call it Gravy?"
ITALIAN-AMERICAN FOOD SPEAK

To many, we Italian-Americans have our own argot. We use a colorful, often confusing shorthand—"*Goombah* this, *oobatz* that, what a *gavone* (i.e., a clod)!" And this especially applies to food. I have heard that Eskimos have fifty words for snow (talk about *oobatz!*). We have five hundred words for food. Here are a few you might hear sitting down to an Italian-American meal.

Gabagool—*The thinly sliced meats you'd find in antipasto or wrapped up as leftovers in the refrigerator. From the Italian* capicola, *boiled ham shaped in a log, usually with a coating of ground hot red pepper.*

Sfogliatell'—*Shorthand for* sfogliatelle, *the classic Neapolitan pastry. Like strudel, multiple layers of thin pastry with a ricotta filling. At its best when eaten warm.*

Gravy—*Tomato sauce, usually the kind made with meat like pork, veal, etc., and typically eaten with macaroni, rigatoni, or ziti. As opposed to marinara sauce, a meatless tomato sauce usually eaten with spaghetti.*

Pasta—*not just spaghetti, fettuccine, etc. Generally, pastry or dough of any kind. When you go into a caffè in Italy, you ask for "una pasta," a pastry.*

Prozhoot'—*Prosciutto, thinly sliced ham, uncooked and unsmoked, often served with sliced melon.*

Moozadell'—*Mozzarella cheese. Buffalo mozzarella is a richer, more complex cheese made from the milk of water buffaloes.*

Giambott'—*Short for* giambotta *or* ciambotta, *a vegetable stew with eggplant, tomato, onion, potatoes, and zucchini, among other things. Also slang for a big mix-up or mess.*

Gavadeel—*Slang for cavatelli, a chewy, shell-shaped pasta common in Southern Italy.*

Zabaglion'—*Zabaglione, a warm, foamy custard made of eggs, sugar, and Marsala wine. A dessert, a sauce for cake, and sometimes comfort food for the sick and ailing.*

Caponata—*A sweet-and-sour eggplant stew.*

Torrone—*A traditional candy, often served at Christmas, either nougat or praline-textured with nuts, usually almonds.*

Fazool—*As in,* pasta fazool. *Formally,* pasta e fagioli *or* fasule, *or pasta and beans, a major Italian comfort food.*

Mesclun—*As in, mesclun salad. Actually, French for wild baby greens, but now popular in all households, including I-A.*

Ziti—*Translated, means "bridegroom," a medium-sized tubular pasta perfect for chunky sauces and meat dishes.*

Rigaton'—*Large grooved pasta with ridges and holes that suck up the sauce.*

Manicott'—*Any dish featuring manicotti, translated, "small muffs," pasta shells often filled with meat, cheese, and vegetables, topped with a sauce, and baked.*

Panacott'—*From panna cotta, cooked vanilla-flavored cream to serve with fruit for dessert.*

Pootsie—*My favorite word for bad food, like "California pizza." Actually, "feces." From "che puzzo," or "what a stink."*

"Una bella mangiata"—*A feed, a bellyful, a good meal. Imagine an Italian man pushing himself away from the table, patting his belly, and exclaiming, "una bella mangiata!"*

Spiedini—*A mozzarella-skewered toasted sandwich or a little roll of thin-sliced veal or pork cutlets with a filling. From* spiedo, *a skewer.*

'Shcarole—*Escarole, a dark leafy green with a slightly bitter taste often used in soups, with beans, and as a side dish with garlic and oil.*

Trippa de zia—*"Your aunt's tripe." Not exactly a food term, but an expression similar to "your sister's ass," i.e., "that's not accurate" or "that's not true."*

How to Cut a Garlic

There are three ways to use garlic in cooking:

1. *For a mild garlic taste, use it whole. Smack it with the flat side of a knife to open it up, and put it in the oil. Some fish the clove out before serving the dish.*

2. *For a medium garlic taste, i.e., in sautéing, slice it razor-thin. You don't need to use a razor, but you get the point.*

3. *For maximum garlic flavor, finely chop it so that it disperses throughout the food.*

Two final points: Avoid garlic presses. Avoid dried garlic powder—that's mayonnaiser behavior.

appointment, without fail, and, if my schedule permits, also to church on Sunday.

Though she has lived in the same little house in Nutley for almost thirty years, the next stop for Ma is a rest home. Hopefully, I can afford to put her in the best of the best. But wherever she is, come Saturday morning, rain or shine, her Paulie will be there to take her shopping and come back and fix her a feast. It's the least I can do after all she has done for me. *Grazie, e che Dio ti benedica, Regina Nucci.*

Zuppa di Scarola e Fagioli

'Shcarole and Beans Soup

Serves 4

1 medium head escarole (about 1 pound)

2 garlic cloves, finely chopped

1/3 cup olive oil

2 medium ripe tomatoes, chopped, or 1 cup chopped canned Italian peeled
   tomatoes

4 cups chicken or beef broth, preferably homemade (or use water)

3 cups cooked or canned cannellini or Great Northern beans

1 cup elbow macaroni or small shells

Salt and freshly ground pepper

1/4 cup freshly grated Pecorino Romano or Parmigiano-Reggiano

✿ ✿ ✿

Trim off the base of the escarole and discard any bruised leaves. Wash the leaves in several changes of cold water, paying special attention to the central ribs where soil tends to collect. Stack the leaves and cut crosswise into 1-inch strips.

In a large pot, cook the garlic in the olive oil over medium-low heat until golden. Add the escarole and tomatoes. Cover and cook for 20 minutes, or until the escarole is tender.

Add the broth and beans and cook for 20 minutes. Stir in the elbows and season to taste with salt and pepper. Cook 10 minutes more, or until the pasta is tender.

Just before serving, sprinkle with the cheese.

Carciofi Ripieni

Stuffed Artichokes

—〰—

Serves 8
8 medium artichokes
3/4 cup plain bread crumbs
1/4 cup chopped fresh flat-leaf parsley
1/4 cup freshly grated Pecorino Romano or Parmigiano-Reggiano
1 garlic clove, very finely chopped
Salt and freshly ground pepper
About 1/4 cup olive oil

——————— ❖ ❖ ❖ ———————

With a large knife, trim off the top 1 inch of the artichokes. Rinse them well under cold water. Cut off the stems so that the artichokes can stand upright. Peel off the tough outer skin of the stems and set them aside.

Bend back and snap off the small leaves around the base of each artichoke. With scissors, trim the pointed tops off the remaining leaves. Removing the choke is optional—if desired, use a small knife with a rounded tip to scrape out the fuzzy leaves in the center.

Finely chop the artichoke stems. Mix the stems in a bowl with the bread crumbs, parsley, cheese, garlic, and salt and pepper to taste. Add a little oil and toss to moisten the crumbs evenly.

Gently spread the artichoke leaves apart and lightly stuff the artichokes with the bread crumb mixture. Place the artichokes in a pot just wide enough to hold them upright. Add water to come to a depth of 3/4 inch around the artichokes.

Drizzle the artichokes with 3 tablespoons olive oil. Cover the pot and place over medium heat. When the water comes to a simmer, reduce the heat to low. Cook until the artichoke bottoms are tender when pierced with a knife and a leaf pulls out easily, about 45 minutes. Add additional warm water if necessary to prevent scorching.

Serve warm or at room temperature.

Uova in Purgatorio

Eggs in Purgatory

—∽—

Serves 4

1 garlic clove, lightly crushed
2 tablespoons olive oil
2 cups canned tomato puree
4 fresh basil leaves, torn into pieces, or a pinch of dried oregano
Salt and freshly ground pepper
8 large eggs
1 tablespoon freshly grated Parmigiano-Reggiano or Pecorino Romano

——— ✿ ✿ ✿ ———

In a medium skillet, cook the garlic in the oil over medium heat for about 2 minutes, or until lightly golden. Add the tomato, basil, and salt and pepper to taste. Bring to a simmer and cook for 15 minutes, or until the sauce is thickened. Discard the garlic.

Break an egg into a small cup. With a spoon, make a well in the tomato sauce. Slide the egg into the sauce. Continue with the remaining eggs. Sprinkle with the cheese. Cover and cook for 3 minutes, or until the eggs are done to taste. Serve hot.

Pork Chops with Vinegar Peppers

—〰—

Serves 4

1 tablespoon olive oil
4 pork rib chops, about 1 inch thick
Salt and freshly ground pepper
2 garlic cloves, lightly crushed
2 cups sliced mild pickled peppers, with 2 tablespoons of their juice (add a
  few hot peperoncini if you like)

——————— ✿ ✿ ✿ ———————

Heat the oil in a large skillet over medium-high heat. When the oil is very hot, pat the chops dry with paper towels. Sprinkle with salt and pepper. Cook the chops, turning once, for about 5 minutes on each side, or until browned.

Lower the heat to medium and scatter the garlic around the chops. Cover the pan. Cook for 5 to 8 minutes more, or until the chops are just slightly pink when cut near the bone. Do not overcook, or the chops will be dry. Transfer the chops to a plate and keep warm.

Add the peppers and the 2 tablespoons liquid to the skillet. Cook, stirring, for 1 to 2 minutes, or until the peppers are just heated through. Spoon the peppers over the chops and serve immediately.

Potatoes and Eggs Sandwiches

—◊◊◊—

Serves 4

3 medium potatoes, peeled
1/4 cup olive oil
Salt
8 large eggs, beaten
Freshly ground pepper
1 loaf Italian bread

———————— ✿ ✿ ✿ ————————

Cut the potatoes in half. Slice each half into 1/4-inch-thick slices.

Pour the oil into a large skillet. Heat over medium heat until the oil sizzles when a piece of potato is added. Pat the potato slices dry and place them in the skillet. Cook, turning the pieces frequently, until the potatoes are browned and tender, about 10 minutes. Sprinkle with salt.

Beat the eggs with salt and pepper to taste. Pour the eggs over the potatoes. When the eggs have begun to set, turn the potato and egg mixture. Cook, turning the potatoes and eggs occasionally, until the eggs are done to taste.

Cut a lengthwise slit in the bread and pull out the soft crumb from the center. Fill the bread with the potatoes and eggs. Cut the loaf into 4 sandwiches. Serve hot or warm.

Peppers and Eggs Sandwiches
—m—

Serves 4
3 tablespooons olive oil
1 large red bell pepper, cored, seeded, and cut into 1-inch pieces
1 large green bell pepper, cored, seeded, and cut into 1-inch pieces
Salt
8 large eggs
Freshly ground pepper
1 long loaf Italian or French bread

——————— ✿ ✿ ✿ ———————

In a large nonstick skillet, heat the oil over medium heat. Add the peppers and salt to taste. Stir the peppers and cook, stirring often, for 15 minutes, or until they are browned. Cover and cook for 5 minutes more, or until the peppers are very tender.

Beat the eggs with salt and pepper to taste. Pour the eggs over the peppers and let them set briefly. Turn the peppers and eggs, to allow the uncooked eggs to reach the bottom of the pan. Allow the eggs to set and stir again. Repeat the stirring and cooking until the eggs are done to taste.

Cut a lengthwise slit in the bread and pull out the soft crumb from the center. Fill the bread with the peppers and eggs. Cut the loaf into 4 sandwiches. Serve hot or warm.

Fried Veal Cutlets

—✿—

Serves 4
2 large eggs
1/2 cup freshly grated Parmigiano-Reggiano
Salt and freshly ground pepper
1 cup plain bread crumbs
1 pound veal, chicken, or turkey cutlets
Vegetable oil
Lemon wedges

——————— ✿ ✿ ✿ ———————

In a shallow plate, beat the eggs with the cheese and salt and pepper to taste. Spread the bread crumbs on a sheet of wax paper.

Dip each piece of the veal in the egg mixture, then in the bread crumbs to coat it completely. Let dry for 15 minutes.

Pour 1/4 inch of oil into a deep heavy skillet. Heat over medium heat until a small drop of the egg mixture sizzles and cooks quickly when dropped into the skillet. Add only as many cutlets to the pan as will fit comfortably in a single layer. Cook, turning once, until golden brown on both sides, about 5 minutes. Transfer the cutlets to a plate lined with paper towels to drain. Continue cooking the remaining cutlets in the same way.

If there is any egg mixture left over after all the cutlets have been coated, stir in some bread crumbs until the mixture holds a soft shape. Fry the egg cutlet, turning once, until golden brown and cooked through. Serve the cutlets hot with lemon wedges.

Neapolitan-Style Stuffed Peppers

—〜〜—

Serves 6

2 medium eggplants
6 large red, yellow, or green bell peppers
1/2 cup plus 3 tablespoons olive oil
3 medium tomatoes, peeled, seeded, and chopped
3/4 cup pitted and chopped black olives, such as Gaeta or oil-cured olives
6 anchovy fillets, finely chopped
3 tablespoons rinsed and drained capers
1 large garlic clove, finely chopped
3 tablespoons chopped fresh flat-leaf parsley
Freshly ground pepper
1/2 cup plus 1 tablespoon plain bread crumbs

————— ✿ ✿ ✿ —————

Trim the eggplants and cut them into 3/4-inch cubes. Layer them in a colander, sprinkling each layer with salt. Place the colander over a plate and let drain for 1 hour.

Preheat the oven to 450°F. Oil a baking pan just large enough to hold the peppers upright.

With a small knife, cut out the stems of the peppers and remove the seeds and white membranes.

Rinse the eggplant and pat dry with paper towels.

In a large skillet, heat the 1/2 cup oil over medium heat. Add the eggplant and cook, stirring occasionally, until tender, about 10 minutes.

Stir in the tomatoes, olives, anchovies, capers, garlic, parsley, and pepper to taste. Bring to a simmer and cook for 5 minutes. Stir in the 1/2 cup bread crumbs and remove from the heat.

Stuff the eggplant mixture into the peppers. Stand the peppers in the prepared pan. Sprinkle with the remaining 1 tablespoon bread crumbs and drizzle with the remaining 3 tablespoons oil.

Pour 1 cup water around the peppers. Bake for 1 hour, or until the peppers are tender and lightly browned. Serve hot or at room temperature.

CHRISTOPHER MOLTISANTI AND ADRIANA LA CERVA

CHAPTER NINE

Cibo D'Amore

ADVICE FROM ADRIANA LA CERVA

Adriana La Cerva was the beautiful hostess at Nuovo Vesuvio for two wonderful years. Her sparkling smile and innate grasp of reservation and seating etiquette garnered her multiple "Employee of the Month" awards. She brought a touch of class, not to mention the blush of youth. Now pursuing a career in club ownership and booking, Adriana nevertheless graciously agreed to give us some of her "inside tips" on Italian-American cuisine that can kindle the flames of passion and romance —cibo d'amore. ❖

Good food is the nectar of the gods and can also be the nectar of a romantic evening with that special someone. Because I am still in my prime dating years—though I am now engaged to a wonderful man, Christopher Moltisanti—many young women approach me about where to go and what to order when their boyfriend announces, "Hey, let's go out to eat." A meal of barbecued ribs and Tater Tots or, say, Kung Pao chicken, I've found, can ruin a chance at love. The MSG alone will kill your desire.

As I always say, make the food fit the mood. First of all, the evening must be special—a birthday, a job promotion, Super Bowl Eve, or maybe a new dress you're longing to wear. Once your beau has agreed to stepping out, immediately *take charge*—you choose the restaurant, make the reservation, and set the dress code—usually Hugo Boss for Chris, Versace for me. If you meet with resistance, as you often will, try to conjure up a picture of a sophisticated evening with an exciting romantic conclusion. I often use that scene from *Goodfellas* where Ray Liotta sweeps Lorraine Bracco through the kitchen and into the Copacabana. Who doesn't want to be a suave man-about-town like Ray Liotta? Think up your own movie image, perhaps from *Pretty Woman*. And be sure to smell like a pretty woman.

Music is very important. Slip something romantic into the car CD player on the way there—I like "Al Green's Greatest Hits," but your tastes could be "old school," like Dean Martin, or more contemporary, like Sade. Hopefully the restaurant will carry forward this erotic soundtrack. If they have a roving Italian trio, all the better. Their whole repertoire is love songs sung in the *real* language of love. You can't miss.

Next, let Mr. Suave choose the wine. If he doesn't know a Chianti from a Coke, gently help him out, but let him make the order. It builds confidence. Now comes my most important piece of advice: *eat light.* Nothing can nullify a romantic evening faster than a full stomach and the heartburn that inevitably follows. I am no dietician, but I find that protein enhances the promise of a long night and that heavy carbs—twice-baked potatoes, for instance, or chocolate cheesecake—tend to make you sluggish, sleepy, and not equipped for strenuous activity. Men often go for red meat, a habit you should encourage. Pasta is always good, of course, but forget the cream sauce. It's bad for business, if you catch my drift.

You now have had the subtle sway of the sexy dress, the perfume, the music, the wine, and a sensuous but not stomach-stuffing meal of the many tastes of Italy. Assuming the chemistry is right—and Lover Boy's credit card doesn't get kicked back—you are on your way. From here on out, I think you can handle the situation. *Buon amante!*

Chris Moltisanti's Favorite Mob Movie Food Scenes

10. *GODFATHER I* When Corleone henchmen Clemenza and Rocco whack the two-faced Paulie out in the Meadowlands and Clemenza says, "Leave the gun. Take the cannoli."

9. *SCARFACE* When Tony Montana (Al Pacino) blows away the sleazy Frank Lopez while Frank drinks Jack Daniels and thinks he just killed Tony. "Manolo," says Tony, "shoot dat piece of chit!"

8. *GODFATHER I* In a little Italian joint, Michael goes to the bathroom, grabs a gun, and then shoots McCloskey the corrupt cop and Sollozo "The Turk" right between the eyes. The cop's face hits the pasta, splat!

7. *YOU BARK, I BITE* (unproduced screenplay) Where Frankie, the main guy, is having dinner with a Spanish punk named Ricardo who had previously plugged Frankie's girlfriend, Angelina, and Ricardo knows Frankie is about to waste him, and he's so nervous that he starts to upchuck the veal right at the table, and Frankie wastes him anyway.

6. *GOODFELLAS* When Joe Pesci, Robert DeNiro, and Ray Liotta go to Pesci's mom's house to get a shovel to bury Billy Batts. Pesci tells his mom he needs a knife because he hit a deer—"a hoof got caught in the grill"—and she insists on fixing them a full pasta dinner in the middle of the night. Great stuff.

5. *A BRONX TALE* When C's dad (DeNiro again) walks up to Sonny the cool mob guy while he's drinking espresso in the back of the bar and tells him to stay away from his son and stop giving him money. Fat chance. As C later tells Dad, "The working man's a sucker!"

4. *LITTLE CAESAR* Opening scene, where Rico (Edward G. Robinson) tells his buddy Joe about hitting it big over "spaghetti and coffee for two."

3. *GOODFELLAS* When the boys are in prison, living like kings. Paulie the boss slices garlic with a razor while Vinnie makes the gravy with too many onions and Ray Liotta takes drugs.

2. *GOODFELLAS* Where Tommy DeVito (Pesci), hanging out with his friends, smashes a glass against club owner Sonny Bunz's head for hassling him about his seven-thousand-dollar bar tab.

1. *PUBLIC ENEMY* When James Cagney stuffs a half a grapefruit smack in Mae Clark's face. Maybe the best use of food in a movie ever.

Risotto with Truffles and Champagne

—〰—

Serves 2

2 cups beef broth
3 cups water
3 tablespoons unsalted butter
1 tablespoon olive oil
1/4 cup minced shallots or onion
1 cup medium-grain rice, such as Arborio or Carnaroli
1/2 cup Champagne or dry white wine
Salt and freshly ground pepper
1 fresh white or black truffle, or use a jarred truffle

——————— ✿ ✿ ✿ ———————

In a saucepan, combine the broth and water, bring to a simmer, and keep warm over very low heat.

In a deep wide saucepan or skillet, melt 2 tablespoons of the butter with the oil over medium heat. Add the shallots and cook for 5 minutes, or until softened but not browned.

Add the rice and stir for 1 minute. Add the Champagne and cook, stirring, until most of the liquid is absorbed. Add 1/2 cup of the broth and cook, stirring, until the liquid is absorbed. Continue cooking, adding the broth 1/2 cup at a time and stirring until it is absorbed, for 18 to 20 minutes, or until the rice is al dente, tender yet firm to the bite. If you are using a jarred truffle, add the liquid from the jar to the rice. About halfway through the cooking time, add salt and pepper to taste. The rice should be moist and creamy. Add more liquid if necessary; if you run out of broth, use water.

If using a fresh truffle, spoon onto plates, then with a truffle shaver or vegetable peeler, shave the truffle over the risotto. If using a jarred truffle, chop it fine and stir it into the risotto. Stir in the remaining 1 tablespoon butter. Serve immediately.

Linguine al Pesto

Serves 2 as a main dish, 4 as a first course
1/2 cup tightly packed fresh basil leaves, rinsed and dried
1 tablespoon pine nuts or blanched almonds
1 garlic clove
Coarse salt
3 tablespoons extra virgin olive oil
1/3 cup freshly grated Parmigiano-Reggiano
1 tablespoon unsalted butter, softened
Salt
8 ounces linguine

❖ ❖ ❖

In a mortar with a pestle, pound the basil with the pine nuts, garlic, and a pinch of coarse salt until the mixture forms a paste. Gradually add the olive oil and continue to blend until smooth. Transfer the mixture to a bowl. Stir in the cheese and butter. (The pesto can also be made in a food processor.)

Bring at least 4 quarts water to a boil in a large pot. Add salt to taste and the pasta and cook, stirring frequently, until the linguine is al dente, tender yet firm to the bite. Drain the pasta, reserving about 1/2 cup of the cooking water.

Place the pasta in a large heated serving bowl. Add the pesto and toss well, adding the reserved pasta water as necessary to loosen the pesto. Serve immediately.

Filet Mignon with Red Wine Sauce

—m—

Serves 2

2 tablespoons unsalted butter
1 teaspoon olive oil
2 filet mignon steaks, about 1 inch thick
Salt and freshly ground pepper

Sauce
2 tablespoons minced shallots or green onions
1 cup dry red wine, such as Barbera
1 tablespoon unsalted butter

--------------- ✿ ✿ ✿ ---------------

In a medium skillet, melt the butter with the oil over high heat. Pat the steaks dry and place them in the skillet. Cook for 1 1/2 to 2 minutes on each side for rare. Sprinkle with salt and pepper and transfer the steaks to hot serving plates.

Pour off most of the fat in the pan. Add the shallots and cook for 1 minute. Add the wine and bring to a simmer. Cook, scraping the bottom of the pan, until the wine is reduced and slightly syrupy. Remove from the heat and swirl in the remaining 1 tablespoon butter.

Spoon the sauce over the steaks and serve immediately.

Shrimp Scampi

—∿—

Serves 2
4 tablespoons unsalted butter
2 tablespoons olive oil
3 large garlic cloves, minced
16 large shrimp, shelled and deveined
Pinch of salt
2 tablespoons very finely chopped fresh flat-leaf parsley, plus a few sprigs
   for garnish
1 tablespoon fresh lemon juice
Lemon wedges

———————— ❖ ❖ ❖ ————————

In a large skillet, melt the butter with the olive oil over medium-low heat. When the butter foam subsides, stir in the garlic. Cook, stirring occasionally, until the garlic is lightly golden, about 7 minutes. Do not let the garlic brown.

Increase the heat to medium-high and add the shrimp and salt. Cook for 2 to 3 minutes, turning the shrimp once, until they are just pink. Stir in the parsley and lemon juice and cook 1 minute more.

Serve garnished with lemon wedges and parsley sprigs.

Veal Scaloppine Marsala

—ᴍ—

Serves 2

8 ounces veal (or thin-sliced chicken) cutlets
Salt and freshly ground pepper
1/3 cup all-purpose flour
2 tablespoons unsalted butter
2 tablespoons vegetable oil
6 ounces mushrooms, trimmed and thinly sliced
1/2 cup dry Marsala

———— ✿ ✿ ✿ ————

Place the cutlets between two sheets of plastic wrap. Using a meat pounder or mallet, pound them gently to about a 1/4-inch thickness. Sprinkle them with salt and pepper. Spread the flour on a piece of wax paper.

In a large skillet, melt 1 tablespoon of the butter with 1 tablespoon of the oil over medium heat. Add the mushrooms and salt and pepper to taste. Cook, stirring often, until the mushrooms are tender and browned, about 10 minutes. Transfer the mushrooms to a plate.

Add the remaining 1 tablespoon each butter and oil to the skillet. When the butter is melted, dip only as many scaloppine in the flour as will fit in the pan in a single layer, then lay the slices in the pan. Cook the veal until nicely browned on both sides, about 1 minute per side. Transfer the slices to the plate with the mushrooms. Repeat with the remaining veal.

When all of the veal has been browned, add the Marsala to the skillet. Cook, stirring, until the wine is reduced and thickened.

Return the veal and mushrooms to the pan. Cook very briefly, turning the veal in the sauce to warm through. Serve hot.

Zabaglione

—✳✳✳—

Serves 2

3 large egg yolks
3 tablespoons sugar
3 tablespoons dry Marsala
Strawberries or raspberries (optional)

——————— ✿ ✿ ✿ ———————

In a medium saucepan, or the bottom half of a double boiler, bring about 2 inches of water to a simmer.

In a heatproof bowl that fits comfortably over the saucepan, or the top half of the double boiler, beat the egg yolks, sugar, and Marsala with a hand-held electric mixer until well blended. Place over the simmering water—do not allow the water to boil. Beat the egg mixture until it is pale yellow and very fluffy, 3 to 5 minutes. Serve immediately, with fresh berries, if desired.

ANTHONY SOPRANO

CHAPTER TEN

Grilling—Italian Style

BY ANTHONY SOPRANO (AS TOLD TO ARTIE BUCCO)

*M*y friend Tony Soprano is both camera-shy and print-shy and respectfully declined to add his own chapter to this epic. Nevertheless, I figured out a way of slipping him in anyway. He's too modest to say so, but Tony is a maestro of the outdoor barbecue grill. Having stood at his side for many a backyard banquet, I've slowly learned his style, his technique, his "filosofia della griglia." With this cookbook in the offing, I began to rush home and take copious notes after every delicious outing. I trust there is no better authority, at least in northern New Jersey, on the art and science of grilling Italian-style. ✿

Grilling, as Tony often points out, is almost genetically a masculine activity, though it takes neither excessive brawn nor brain. Cooking outside, especially cooking meat, awakens a primitive tribal instinct in men. It involves all the stuff of early civilization—fire, freshly killed animals, and a long stick (or fork) for poking raw flesh. Tofu be damned, there will never be an acceptable "meat substitute" for the Tony Sopranos of the world.

Grilling is simple, Tony contends, if you know what you're doing. Most people don't. They soak a bagful of discount briquettes with lighter fluid and cook a pork chop until it's shoe leather and think they're Wolfgang Puck.

Here's Tony's checklist of rudimentary grilling do's and don'ts.

THE FIRE: Use hardwood charcoal pieces rather than briquettes. They burn better. Heat them up with newspaper or an electric starter, unless you're particularly fond of the taste of gasoline. Tony likes to add aromatic wood chips like mesquite for extra flavor. His mother used to hate the taste of mesquite, but she was not an adventurous person. Tony soaks his chips in water for thirty minutes or so before using them. They burn more slowly

Tony is "down" on liquid lighter fluids and accelerants. A faulty can of such material almost caused him serious injury—and at his son's birthday party yet.

and the moisture ensures more smoke to flavor the meat.

THE GRILL: Place the grill rack the correct distance from the coals. It sounds obvious, but most grillers don't do this and end up with inedible results. The slower the cooking time, the further the distance. For chicken with the bone still in, set the rack five or six inches off the fire. A steak cooks faster, so move it closer, say, two or three inches above.

Artie on Italian Sausage

Just because it says "Italian" doesn't mean it is Italian. The best Italian sausage does not include turkey, chicken, sun-dried tomatoes, or any other designer ingredients. It's pork, the meat of pigs. It can be "sweet," with black pepper and/or fennel, or it can be "hot," with crushed red pepper. Get it fresh from a butcher—Satriale's, if you live in the area.

You can tell a good sausage by looking at it—it's plump pink meat with just the right amount of fat. Too much fat, it's greasy; too little, it's dry. Ask the butcher for the right selection. That's his job.

Finally, don't buy the packaged sausage from the supermarket. Who knows what's in it? Sure, it says "Low-Cal Turkey Sausage with Basil, Oregano, and Bing Cherries," but what part of the turkey? Ponder that.

THE HEAT: Here's one of Tony's patented tricks: To gauge the heat of the coals, hold your open hand six inches above them. Then start counting. If you can last only one or two seconds before cursing, then the fire is very hot. Three or four seconds means it's medium-hot, and five or six seconds means the heat factor is low. Of course, for some things, like grilling vegetables, you might want a low heat factor. It's tricky—half the time even Tony burns the eggplant.

COOKING: This is the true "art" of outdoor grilling. There is no set cooking time

for chicken, pork, or a rib-eye steak. Depending on how you prepare the dish (this is where the "Italian-style" comes in), the level of heat, or the position of the grill, for instance, a sparerib could take three minutes or thirty seconds. Almost every griller freaks out and overcooks the meat. Don't do this. Pay attention to what you're doing and save your guests from gagging on cardboard cutlets.

Tony uses tongs to handle the food, not a fork or his fingers, and he keeps a spray bottle of water close by to squelch any flare-ups that might occur.

Finally, watch the alcohol while grilling. If you're knocking back J & B's, everything will come out black, dry, and tasteless. I know that many of you think that's what all charcoal cuisine tastes like—like charcoal—but that's only because the grillmaster in question is an amateur. Grilled food can be *magnifico*. Settle for nothing less.

Junior's Ten Tips to Living Long and Living Well

As it is well known, eating grilled red meat for years at a time can kill you. But some of us survive despite our artery-clogging dining habits. Junior Soprano is one such survivor. Here are a few of his tips for staying alive.—AB

1. *Always trust blood relatives over friends, but not very far.*

2. *Learn to sing. It's impossible to sing and be pissed off at the same time.*

3. *Have lunch with friends at least three times a week. If they resist, insist.*

4. *Never feel guilty about anything. If it happened, it happened. Just go on.*

5. *Red wine is rich in iron and an effective antispasmodic. If possible, drink it at every meal except breakfast.*

6. *Eat at least one bowl of spaghetti a day. Breakfast (cold) is deelish!*

7. *If a man should insult you, do not be quick to return the insult. Wait and prepare. The best comeback is like a wrong number at three in the morning—very disturbing.*

8. *The only lesson my father ever taught me—kick the shit out of the other guy before he kicks the shit out of you.*

9. *To quote my dear brother Johnny: enjoy the music of life while you still have ears.*

10. *Rule of rules: never whine. No one cares.*

Verdure alla Griglia

Grilled Vegetables

Serves 8

1 medium eggplant, trimmed and cut into 1/2-inch-thick slices
Salt
1 large red or Spanish onion, cut into 1/2-inch-thick slices
4 large mushrooms, such as portobello, stems removed
4 medium tomatoes, cored and cut crosswise in half
2 large red or yellow bell peppers, cored, seeded, and cut into quarters
Olive oil
Freshly ground pepper
6 fresh basil leaves, torn into bits

Sprinkle the eggplant slices generously with salt. Place the slices in a colander and let drain over a plate for 30 to 60 minutes. Rinse the slices and pat dry.

Prepare a medium hot charcoal fire or preheat a gas grill or the broiler. Place the grill rack or broiler pan 4 inches from the heat.

Generously brush all the vegetables with olive oil and sprinkle with salt and pepper. Place the vegetables on the grill or broiler pan. Cook, turning once, until tender and browned, about 15 minutes. If the vegetables are getting too browned before they are done, move them to a cooler spot.

Arrange the vegetables on a platter and sprinkle with additional oil and the basil. Serve hot or at room temperature.

Salsiccie alla Griglia

Grilled Sausages

—◊◊◊—

Serves 6

2 pounds assorted Italian pork sausages, such as sweet, hot, parsley-and-
   cheese, fennel, and cervelat

———— ✿ ✿ ✿ ————

Prepare a medium-hot charcoal fire or preheat a gas grill or the broiler. Place the grill rack or broiler pan 4 inches from the heat.

Place the sausages on the grill and cook, turning them once or twice, until browned and cooked through. Use tongs to turn the sausages and be careful not to pierce their skins, or the juices will run out and cause flare-ups. Serve hot.

Tonno alla Griglia

Tuna Steaks with Lemon and Oregano

—∾∾—

Serves 4
4 tuna steaks, about 1 inch thick, trimmed
Olive oil
Salt and freshly ground pepper
1 tablespoon lemon juice
1/2 teaspoon dried oregano

──────── ✿ ✿ ✿ ────────

Prepare a medium-hot charcoal fire or preheat a gas grill or the broiler. Place the grill rack or broiler pan 4 inches from the heat.

Generously brush the tuna steaks with oil and season with salt and pepper to taste.

Grill the tuna, turning once, until browned but still pink inside, about 5 minutes.

In a small bowl, whisk together 3 tablespoons olive oil, the lemon juice, oregano, and salt and pepper to taste. Pour the lemon juice mixture over the tuna steaks and serve immediately.

Rollatine di Pesce Spada

Swordfish Rolls

Serves 6

1 1/2 pounds swordfish, skin removed and cut into very thin slices

3/4 cup plain bread crumbs

2 tablespoons chopped drained capers

2 tablespoons chopped fresh flat-leaf parsley

1 large garlic clove, minced

Salt and freshly ground pepper

1/4 cup olive oil

2 tablespoons fresh lemon juice

Lemon wedges

Prepare a medium-hot fire in a charcoal grill or preheat a gas grill or the broiler. Place the grill rack or broiler pan 4 inches from the heat.

Place the swordfish slices between two sheets of plastic wrap. Using a meat pounder or a mallet, gently pound the slices to an even 1/4-inch thickness. Cut the fish into 3 x 2-inch pieces.

In a bowl, combine the bread crumbs, capers, parsley, garlic, and salt and pepper to taste. Add 3 tablespoons of the oil and mix until the crumbs are evenly moistened.

Place a tablespoon of the crumb mixture at one narrow end of each piece of fish, roll up the fish, and fasten it closed with a toothpick.

Whisk together the lemon juice and the remaining 1 tablespoon oil. Brush the mixture over the rolls. Sprinkle the fish with any remaining bread crumb mixture, patting it so that it adheres.

Grill the rolls for 3 to 4 minutes on each side, or until they are browned and feel firm when pressed in the center. They should still be slightly rare. Serve hot with lemon wedges.

Bistecca Fiorentina

Steak Florentine-Style

—ɱ—

Serves 6 to 8
2 porterhouse steaks (about 2 pounds each), about 1 1/2 inches thick
Salt and freshly ground pepper
Extra virgin olive oil
Lemon wedges

———— ✤ ✤ ✤ ————

Prepare a medium-hot charcoal fire or preheat a gas grill or the broiler. Place the grill rack or broiler pan 4 inches from the heat.

Rub the steaks all over with salt and pepper. Grill or broil for 4 to 5 minutes, depending on the thickness of the steaks, on each side, for rare. Make a small cut in the thickest part and check the center for doneness. For longer cooking, move the steaks to a cooler part of the grill.

Let the steaks rest for 5 minutes before cutting into thin slices. Sprinkle with more salt and drizzle with oil. Serve with lemon wedges.

Spiedini

Stuffed Veal Rolls

—∿—

Serves 6

1 1/2 pounds veal cutlets
Salt and freshly ground pepper
8 ounces fresh mozzarella
3 tablespoons chopped fresh flat-leaf parsley
2 garlic cloves, minced
3 tablespoons olive oil
3/4 cup plain bread crumbs

✿ ✿ ✿

Prepare a medium-hot charcoal fire or preheat a gas grill or the broiler. Place the grill rack or broiler pan 4 inches from the heat.

Place the cutlets between two sheets of plastic wrap. Using a meat pounder or mallet, pound them gently to a 1/4-inch thickness.

Cut the veal into 3 x 2-inch pieces. Sprinkle with salt and pepper. Cut the mozzarella into 1 x 1/2-inch-thick sticks. Place a piece of cheese across the center of each veal cutlet. Sprinkle with the parsley and garlic. Roll up each piece of veal from one of the short sides.

Hold two metal or bamboo skewers parallel about 1 inch apart, spear one of the rolls on the skewers, as if they were the tines of a large fork, and push the meat toward the opposite end of the skewers. Leave an inch or two clear at the base for easy handling. Thread a few more rolls on the skewers in the same way; the rolls should be barely touching. Skewer the remaining rolls in the same way.

Brush the rolls with the olive oil and sprinkle with the crumbs, patting them so they adhere. Grill or broil the skewers, turning once, just until the meat is browned and the cheese is slightly melted, about 10 minutes.

Slide the rolls off the skewers onto a heated serving platter. Serve immediately.

Balsamic Grilled Veal Chops

—◊◊◊—

Serves 4

4 veal loin or rib chops, about 1 inch thick
2 tablespoons olive oil
2 tablespoons balsamic vinegar
1 tablespoon minced fresh rosemary
Salt and freshly ground pepper

——————— ✿ ✿ ✿ ———————

Place the chops in a shallow dish and sprinkle them with the oil, vinegar, rosemary, and salt and pepper to taste. Turn them to coat evenly. Let the chops stand at room temperature while you prepare a medium-hot charcoal fire or preheat a gas grill or the broiler.

Set a grill rack or broiler pan about 4 inches from the heat. Grill or broil the chops for 3 to 4 minutes per side for medium-rare. Serve immediately.

Grilled Spareribs

—✃—

Serves 4
1/4 cup olive oil
3 garlic cloves, finely chopped
1 tablespoon chopped fresh sage
1 tablespoon chopped fresh rosemary
Pinch of crushed red pepper
Salt
4 pounds spareribs, cut into individual ribs

————————— ✿ ✿ ✿ —————————

In a shallow dish, combine the oil, garlic, sage, rosemary, red pepper, and salt to taste. Add the ribs and stir them to coat with the marinade. Cover and refrigerate for at least several hours, or overnight.

Prepare a medium-hot charcoal fire or preheat a gas grill or the broiler. Set the rack or broiler pan about 6 inches from the heat.

Grill or broil the ribs, turning them frequently, until browned and cooked through, about 20 minutes. Serve hot.

ROBERT "BOBBY BACALA" BACCALIERI

CHAPTER ELEVEN

If I Couldn't Eat, I'd F**king Die

BOBBY BACALA SPEAKS OUT

Old pal Robert Baccalieri, otherwise known as "Bobby Bacala," loves his food. And at 260 pounds, he wears that love proudly. A business associate of Tony Soprano and a devoted family man, he is shy and reticent in person, surprisingly so given his heft. But he is not shy about voicing some strong opinions about issues that affect us all. He is also a connoisseur of Italian-American desserts, a fitting conclusion to this gastronomic journey. ✿

Thank you, Artie, for giving me this opportunity to speak about something that greatly concerns me. That is the issue of thinness. All one has to do is turn on the TV or pick up a magazine and one can see the obsession this country has with thinness. Thin movie stars, thin models, endless ads for products of thinness. Personally, I think this is a disturbing, even dangerous, trend in our society.

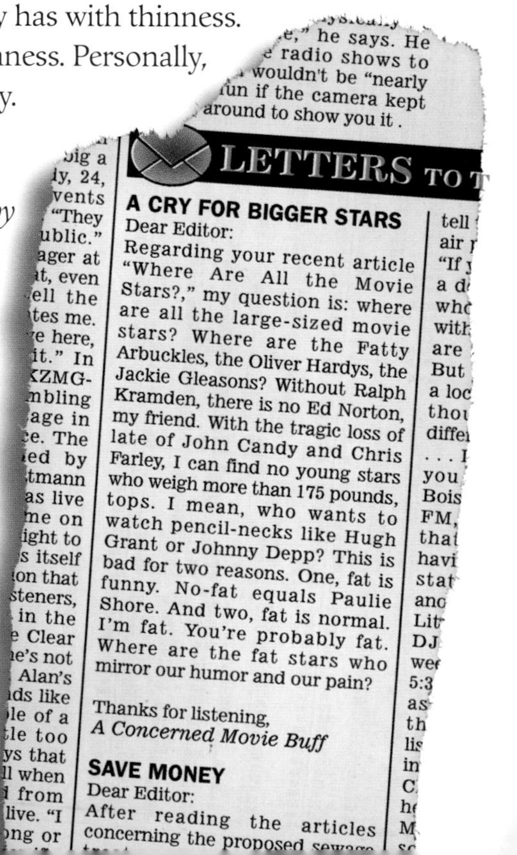

When I was growing up in the Italian-American subculture, being thin was not the end-all of living. Being *happy* was the end-all of living. Being happy meant having a loving and supportive family, a loving and supportive community, and plenty of food on the table. Those are the things that to this day I associate with a contented life: my dear Ma, Mr. Falcone the baker, and *sfogliatell'*. Yet those values are a world away from the values promulgated by today's mass media. Happiness, in their terms, equals wealth, stardom, and thinness. Since few can achieve this rare hat trick in life, most people are left unhappy, and that's not right.

My own kids are of regular size, thank God, but I have a young niece who is on the high end of the scales and I can see

[Newspaper clipping, partially visible:]

"...e," he says. He ... e radio shows to ... wouldn't be "nearly ... un if the camera kept ... around to show you it .

LETTERS TO T...

A CRY FOR BIGGER STARS

Dear Editor:

Regarding your recent article "Where Are All the Movie Stars?," my question is: where are all the large-sized movie stars? Where are the Fatty Arbuckles, the Oliver Hardys, the Jackie Gleasons? Without Ralph Kramden, there is no Ed Norton, my friend. With the tragic loss of late of John Candy and Chris Farley, I can find no young stars who weigh more than 175 pounds, tops. I mean, who wants to watch pencil-necks like Hugh Grant or Johnny Depp? This is bad for two reasons. One, fat is funny. No-fat equals Paulie Shore. And two, fat is normal. I'm fat. You're probably fat. Where are the fat stars who mirror our humor and our pain?

Thanks for listening,
A Concerned Movie Buff

SAVE MONEY
Dear Editor:
After reading the articles concerning the proposed sewage

the misery she experiences daily because of her genetic destiny. My friends don't shun me because I must wear my shirts hanging out, Hawaiian-style, but her friends do. My friends love to get together over a hearty three-course meal and exchange pleasantries, but her friends don't. They get together over yogurt and complain about their weight. Why are we making our young people miserable? Aren't they miserable enough just being young?

Personally, I like to look at a model-thin woman as much as the next guy, but that needn't exclude the many fetching full-figured ones. And why do men, of all people, care to be thin? Who's looking at them? A man positions himself in the world via his courage and manliness, not his waistline. All of my friends know this, even the skinny ones, but many men out there are deluded in their search for masculine perfection. They are barking up the wrong tree of life.

At least that's one man's opinion. Thanks for listening and have a dessert on me. In fact, have two.

The Perfect Cannoli

Given that you can buy what's called a cannoli at every coffee boutique east of Seattle, you should be aware of what a genuine cannoli is supposed to taste like. The shell should be crisp and delicate, not hard or spongy. It should shatter when you cut it. The ricotta cheese filling should be creamy—not grainy or chunky—and should be added at the very last minute to avoid a soggy shell. If the whole thing has been sitting in the display case since Labor Day, go with the biscotti or the day-old donut.

Style Tips for Heavy Eaters

Here are a few quick clothing tips, gathered from large men in the neighborhood, including the always-sartorial Bacala, for guys who like to enjoy food and enjoy life.—AB

1. No tank tops.

2. Black and loose-fitting. You can't go wrong.

3. A colorful shirt that is meant to be worn tail out. Both the Hawaiians and the Mexicans make a good one.

4. Jumpsuits, but not prison-issue orange ones.

5. Velour sweatsuits, for sure, but not baby pink or blue. Maroon or fuchsia are always in style.

6. Any jewelry that announces you are a "fat cat."

7. If you are fat and balding, wear an expensive hat.

8. Italian shoes. Shoes, as they say, make the man.

9. Most importantly: wear what you wear with confidence; if it doesn't make you cocky, don't wear it.

Tiramisu

—ᨓ—

Serves 8

1 pound mascarpone
1/4 cup sugar
2 tablespoons amaretto or Cognac
1 cup heavy cream
24 savoiardi (imported Italian ladyfingers)
1 cup brewed espresso, at room temperature
1/2 cup chopped bittersweet chocolate

————— ✿ ✿ ✿ —————

In a large bowl, whisk together the mascarpone, sugar, and amaretto until smooth.

In a chilled bowl with chilled beaters, whip the cream until soft peaks form. Fold the cream into the mascarpone mixture.

Lightly dip half of the savoiardi in the espresso and arrange them in a single layer in the bottom of an 8-inch square pan. Spread half the mascarpone mixture over the savoiardi. Sprinkle with half the chocolate.

Dip the remaining savoiardi in the espresso. Top with the remaining mascarpone mixture, spreading it smooth. Sprinkle with the remaining chocolate. Cover with plastic wrap. Refrigerate for several hours, or overnight, before serving.

Ricotta Cheesecake

—〰—

Serves 12

3 pounds ricotta cheese

8 large eggs

2 teaspoons vanilla extract

1 teaspoon grated orange zest

1 teaspoon grated lemon zest

1 1/2 cups sugar

1/3 cup cornstarch

❖ ❖ ❖

Preheat the oven to 350°F.

Butter a 9-inch springform pan. Dust the pan with flour and tap out the excess. Place the pan on a 12-inch square of heavy-duty aluminum foil. Mold the foil tightly around the pan so that water cannot seep in.

In a food processor or blender, puree the ricotta until very smooth. Pour the ricotta into a large bowl. Add the eggs, vanilla, and zests and whisk until well blended.

Stir together the sugar and cornstarch. Add to the ricotta mixture and stir until smooth.

Pour the batter into the prepared pan. Place the pan in a large roasting pan and place it on the middle rack of the oven. Carefully pour hot water to come to a depth of 1 inch into the roasting pan. Bake for 1 1/2 hours or until the top of the cheesecake is golden and a knife inserted 2 inches from the center of the cake comes out clean.

Turn off the oven and prop the door open with a wooden spoon. Let the cake cool for 30 minutes in the turned-off oven.

Remove the cake from the roasting pan and remove the foil wrapping. Cool to room temperature on a wire rack.

Serve at room temperature or slightly chilled. Wrap leftovers tightly and store in the refrigerator.

Torta Caprese

Capri Chocolate Almond Cake

—ᘉ—

Serves 10
8 ounces almonds (about 1 1/2 cups)
1/2 pound (2 sticks) unsalted butter, softened
1 cup sugar
6 large eggs, separated, at room temperature
8 ounces semisweet chocolate, melted and cooled
Pinch of salt
Confectioners' sugar
Whipped cream (optional)

———————— ✿ ✿ ✿ ————————

Preheat the oven to 350°F. Butter a 9-inch springform pan. Line the base with wax paper or parchment. Butter the paper and sprinkle it with flour. Tap out the excess.

In a food processor, grind the almonds very fine.

In the large bowl of an electric mixer, beat the butter and 3/4 cup of the sugar on high speed until very light and fluffy, about 5 minutes. Add the egg yolks one at a time, beating well after each addition. Stir in the chocolate and almonds.

In the clean large mixer bowl, beat the egg whites with the salt on low speed until foamy. Increase the speed to high and beat in the remaining 1/4 cup sugar. Continue to beat until the egg whites hold soft peaks when the beaters are lifted.

Fold about one quarter of the whites into the chocolate mixture to lighten it. Gently fold in the remaining whites.

Scrape the batter into the prepared pan. Bake for 45 minutes, or until the cake is set around the edge but still soft and moist in the center. Let cool on a rack for 10 minutes.

Invert the cake onto a cooling rack and peel off the paper. Invert again so that it is right side up. Let cool completely, then dust with confectioners' sugar. Serve with whipped cream, if desired.

Biscotti di Pinoli

Pignoli Cookies

—m—

Makes 30

One 8-ounce can almond paste
2 large egg whites, beaten, plus 1 more if necessary
1 cup confectioners' sugar, plus more for decorating
2 cups pignoli nuts or slivered almonds

————— ✿ ✿ ✿ —————

Preheat the oven to 350° F. Generously butter a large baking sheet.

Crumble the almond paste into the large bowl of an electric mixer. Beat in the 2 egg whites and the confectioners' sugar until smooth. The batter should be very soft and sticky. If it is not, beat the extra egg white and add another tablespoon of egg white.

Place the pignoli nuts in a small bowl. Drop a scant tablespoon of the batter into the nuts and roll it into a ball. Coating the cookies completely with nuts helps prevent them from sticking to the baking sheet. Place the ball on the prepared baking sheet. Repeat with the remaining batter and nuts, placing the balls about 1 inch apart.

Bake for 18 to 20 minutes, or until lightly browned. Let cool for 2 minutes on the pan, then transfer the cookies to racks to cool completely. Dust the cooled cookies with confectioners' sugar. Store in an airtight container or in the freezer up to one month.

Baba au Rhum

Rum Cake

—〰—

Serves 8 to 10

1 package active dry yeast

1/4 cup warm water (105° to 115°F)

6 large eggs, at room temperature

1 tablespoon grated lemon zest

2 2/3 cups all-purpose flour

3 tablespoons sugar

1/2 teaspoon salt

12 tablespoons (1 1/2 sticks) unsalted butter, softened

For the Syrup

2 cups sugar

2 cups water

1/2 cup dark rum

Whipped cream

--------- ✿ ✿ ✿ ---------

Generously butter a 10-inch Bundt or tube pan.

Sprinkle the yeast over the warm water in a measuring cup or a small bowl. Let stand for 1 minute, or until creamy, then stir until dissolved.

In a large mixing bowl, beat the eggs and lemon zest until blended. Beat in the flour, sugar, and salt. Add the yeast and butter and beat until well blended.

Scrape the dough into the prepared pan. Cover with plastic wrap and let stand in a warm place for 1 hour, or until the dough has doubled in volume.

Preheat the oven to 400°F.

Bake the cake for 30 minutes, or until it is golden and a cake tester inserted in the center comes out clean. Invert the cake onto a wire rack to cool for 10 minutes. Set the pan aside.

Meanwhile, to make the syrup, combine the sugar and water in a medium saucepan. Bring to a boil and stir until the sugar is dissolved. Stir in the rum. Remove from the heat, and set aside 1/4 cup of the syrup.

Return the still-hot cake to the pan. With a skewer, poke holes all over the surface. Slowly spoon the hot syrup over the cake.

Just before serving, invert the cake onto a serving plate. Drizzle with the reserved syrup. Serve with whipped cream.

Mille Foglie

Napoleons

—∿—

Serves 8

For the Pastry Cream
2 cups milk
1/4 cup sugar
1/4 cup all-purpose flour
3 large egg yolks
2 teaspoons vanilla extract

1 pound frozen all-butter puff pastry, thawed
Confectioners' sugar

————————— ✿ ✿ ✿ —————————

To make the pastry cream, bring 1 cup of the milk and the sugar to a simmer in a heavy saucepan over medium heat, stirring to dissolve the sugar. Remove from the heat.

In a large heatproof bowl, whisk the egg yolks and the remaining 1 cup milk until blended. Place the flour in a sieve and sift it over the egg yolks, whisking until smooth. Beat in the hot milk a little at a time.

When all of the milk has been added, transfer the mixture to the saucepan and return it to the heat. Cook, stirring constantly, over medium heat until the mixture begins to boil. Reduce the heat and cook for 30 seconds more. Remove the pan from the heat and stir in the vanilla.

Transfer the pastry cream to a bowl. Cover with plastic wrap, pressing the plastic directly against the surface of the cream. Refrigerate until chilled.

On a lightly floured surface, roll out the puff pastry to a 14 x 12-inch rectangle. Place the pastry on a large ungreased baking sheet. Refrigerate for 30 minutes.

Preheat the oven to 400°F.

With a fork, prick the dough all over. Invert an ungreased baking sheet on top of the dough. Bake for 10 minutes. Remove the baking sheet, prick the dough again, and bake 15 to 20 minutes more, or until the pastry is golden brown. Slide the pastry onto a rack and let cool completely.

Place the pastry on a cutting board. With a serrated knife, using a sawing motion, cut the pastry crosswise into 3 equal strips. Place one strip on a serving platter. Spread with half of the pastry cream. Top with a second layer and the remaining pastry cream. Place the remaining layer on top. Refrigerate for up to 4 hours before serving.

Sprinkle the mille foglie generously with confectioners' sugar. With a serrated knife, cut into 1 1/2-inch slices and serve.

Cannoli

—m—

Cannoli tubes are available at kitchenware shops, generally in sets of four. You can reuse them, but it is easier if you have at least eight to work with.

Makes 16

For the Ricotta Cream
2 pounds whole- or part-skim-milk ricotta
1 1/2 cups confectioners' sugar
1 teaspoon vanilla extract
1/2 teaspoon ground cinnamon
1 ounce semisweet chocolate, chopped
2 tablespoons chopped candied orange peel

For the Shells
2 cups all-purpose flour, plus more as needed
1 tablespoon sugar
1 teaspoon unsweetened cocoa powder
1/2 teaspoon ground cinnamon
1/2 teaspoon salt
3 tablespoons vegetable oil
About 1/2 cup dry white wine

1 egg white, beaten
Vegetable oil for deep-frying

Candied cherries or candied orange peel (optional)
Confectioners' sugar

✿ ✿ ✿

Line a large strainer with cheesecloth. Place the strainer over a bowl. Scrape the ricotta into the strainer and cover with a piece of plastic wrap and a small plate. Weight the plate with a heavy can. Let the ricotta drain in the refrigerator for several hours, or overnight.

To make the shells, in the large bowl of an electric mixer, combine the flour, sugar, cocoa, cinnamon, and salt. Stir in the oil and enough wine to make a soft dough. Turn the dough out onto a lightly floured surface and knead it until smooth and well blended, about 2 minutes. Shape the dough into a ball. Cover with plastic wrap and let rest at room temperature for at least 30 minutes.

Cut the dough into 4 pieces. Starting at the middle setting, run one of the pieces of dough through the rollers of a pasta machine. Lightly dust the dough with flour as needed to keep the pieces from sticking. Continue to pass the dough through the machine until you reach the last or second-to-the-last setting. The dough strip should be about 4 inches wide and thin enough to see your hand through. (The dough can be rolled on a board with a rolling pin, but be sure to roll it very thin.) Measure the length of your cannoli tubes and cut the strip of dough crosswise into pieces about 1 inch shorter.

Continue rolling out the remaining dough. If you do not have enough cannoli tubes for all of the dough, lay the pieces of dough on sheets of plastic wrap and keep them covered until you are ready to use them.

Oil the cannoli tubes. Place a cannoli tube on one piece of dough at an angle, from corner to corner. Fold the two other corners of the dough around the tube, being careful not to stretch the dough or pull it tightly. Dab a little egg white on the dough where the edges overlap—avoid getting egg white on the tube, or the cannoli will stick to it. Press the overlap to seal. Repeat with the remaining dough.

Pour 2 inches of oil into a deep fryer or deep heavy saucepan. Heat to 375°F on a deep-frying thermometer. Line a baking pan with paper towels. Carefully lower a few of the cannoli tubes into the hot oil. Do not crowd the pan. Fry the shells until golden, about 2 minutes, turning them so that they brown evenly.

With tongs, remove the cannoli tubes, holding them straight up so that the oil flows back into the pan. Drain the tubes briefly on the paper towels.

While they are still hot, carefully slide the cannoli shells from the tubes: Grasp each tube with a pot holder and pull the cannoli shell off the tube with a pair of tongs, or with your hand protected by an oven mitt or towel. Cool the shells completely on the paper towels.

Repeat with the remaining dough. (If you are reusing the cannoli tubes, let them cool before wrapping them in the dough.) Set aside. (The cannoli shells can be made up to 2 days before serving. Store in a sealed container in a cool, dry place.)

To make the ricotta cream, put the ricotta in a food processor and blend it until creamy. Add the confectioners' sugar, vanilla, and cinnamon and blend until smooth. Transfer to a bowl and stir in the chocolate and the candied fruit, if using. (The filling can be made up to 24 hours before serving. Cover and refrigerate.)

To assemble, fill a pastry bag fitted with a 1/2-inch plain tip, or a heavy-duty plastic storage bag, with the ricotta cream. If using a plastic bag, cut about 1/2 inch off one bottom corner. Insert the tip or the bag in a cannoli shell and squeeze gently until the shell is half-filled. Turn the shell and fill from the other side. Smooth the cream with a small spatula. Repeat with the remaining shells and cream. If desired, decorate the ends with candied cherries or strips of orange peel.

Place the cannoli on a serving platter and sprinkle with confectioners' sugar. Serve within 1 hour.

Bicotti d'Anice

Bishkott'—〰—*Anise Cookies*

Makes about 3 dozen
2 large eggs, at room temperature
2 teaspoons anise extract
1 teaspoon vanilla extract
1/2 cup sugar
1 cup all-purpose flour
2 tablespoons cornstarch
1 teaspoon baking powder
1 teaspoon anise seeds

❖ ❖ ❖

Preheat the oven to 350°F. Butter a 9-inch square baking pan. Line the bottom of the pan with wax paper. Butter and flour the paper. Tap out the excess.

In the large bowl of an electric mixer, combine the eggs, extracts, and sugar. With the whisk attachment or beaters, begin beating the eggs on low speed, gradually increasing the speed to high and continue to whip the eggs for 5 to 7 minutes, until they are very light and foamy and tripled in volume.

Place the flour, cornstarch, and baking powder in a sieve. Shake about one-third of the mixture over the egg mixture. Gently but thoroughly fold in the dry ingredients. Repeat two more times with the remaining flour mixture. Fold in the anise seeds.

Scrape the batter into the prepared pan, leveling the top with a rubber spatula. Bake for 20 to 25 minutes, until the top is evenly browned and firm when touched lightly in the center.

Remove the cake from the oven and run a small knife around the edges. Invert the cake onto a cutting board. Raise the oven temperature to 375°F.

With a long serrated knife, cut the cake into 3 strips. Cut each strip into 3/4-inch-thick slices. Place the slices on a large baking sheet.

Bake the slices for 5 to 10 minutes, or until toasted and golden. Remove them from the oven and let cool on a wire rack. Store in a tightly covered container in a cool, dry place.

Tortoni

Almond Cream Dessert

—✻—

Makes 8
4 to 6 imported Italian amaretti cookies
2 cups heavy cream
1/2 cup confectioners' sugar
1 1/2 teaspoons vanilla extract
1/2 teaspoon almond extract
2 large egg whites
Pinch of salt

——————— ✿ ✿ ✿ ———————

Put the cookies in a small heavy-duty plastic bag and crush them gently with a heavy object. There should be about 1/4 cup crumbs.

Combine the cream, confectioners' sugar, vanilla, and almond extract in a large chilled bowl. Beat with a hand-held electric mixer on high speed until the cream holds soft peaks when the beaters are lifted.

In a clean bowl, with clean beaters, beat the egg whites with the salt on low speed until foamy. Gradually increase the speed and beat until the whites hold soft peaks. Fold the whites into the whipped cream.

Spoon the mixture into eight wine goblets or coffee cups, or use small pleated paper muffin cups. Sprinkle the tortoni with the amaretti crumbs. Cover with plastic wrap and freeze for at least 4 hours, or overnight. Remove from the freezer 15 minutes before serving.

Zeppole

Doughnuts

—〰—

Serves 10 to 12
1 cup warm water (110° to 115°F)
1 teaspoon active dry yeast
1 tablespoon sugar
2 cups all-purpose flour
1 teaspoon salt
Vegetable oil for deep-frying
Confectioners' sugar

——————— ✿ ✿ ✿ ———————

Sprinkle the yeast and sugar over the water in a measuring cup. Stir until the yeast dissolves.

In a large mixing bowl, combine the flour and salt. Add the yeast mixture and stir until well blended. Cover with plastic wrap. Let rise in a warm place for 1 1/2 hours.

Pour about 2 inches of oil into a deep heavy saucepan or deep fryer. Heat the oil until the temperature reaches 375°F on a deep-frying thermometer, or a drop of the dough slipped into the oil sizzles and turns brown in 1 minute.

Drop the dough by tablespoons into the hot oil. Do not crowd the pan. Cook the zeppole until golden brown and puffed, about 2 minutes. Remove the zeppole with a slotted spoon and drain them briefly on paper towels. Repeat with the remaining dough.

Put the zeppole in a paper bag, add the confectioners' sugar, and shake them until well coated. Serve immediately.

Cassata

Cassata Cake

—◊◊◊—

For the Filling
1 pound whole- or part-skim-milk ricotta
1/2 cup confectioners' sugar
1 teaspoon vanilla extract
2 ounces semisweet or bittersweet chocolate, chopped
1/2 cup chopped candied fruit, such as citron or orange peel

For the Sponge Cake
6 large eggs, at room temperature
2/3 cup sugar
1 1/2 teaspoons vanilla extract
1 cup sifted all-purpose flour

4 ounces almond paste
2 or 3 drops green food coloring

For the Icing
2 large egg whites
1/4 teaspoon grated lemon zest
1 tablespoon fresh lemon juice
2 cups confectioners' sugar

Candied or dried fruit, such as cherries, pineapple, or oranges

———— ✜ ✜ ✜ ————

To make the filling, line a large strainer with cheesecloth and place it over a bowl. Scrape the ricotta into the sieve and cover with plastic wrap. Place a plate on top of the ricotta and a heavy object such as a can on the plate. Let the ricotta drain in the refrigerator for several hours, or overnight.

Beat the ricotta, confectioners' sugar, and vanilla in the bowl of an electric mixer until smooth and creamy. Fold in the chocolate and chopped candied fruit. (The filling can be made up to 24 hours ahead. Cover and refrigerate.)

To make the sponge cake, preheat the oven to 375°F. Butter two 9-inch layer cake pans. Line the bottom of the pans with circles of waxed paper or parchment paper. Butter the paper. Dust the pans with flour and tap out the excess.

In the large bowl of an electric mixer, begin beating the eggs on low speed. Slowly add the sugar, gradually increasing the mixer speed to high. Add the vanilla. Beat the eggs until very thick, light, and fluffy, 5 to 7 minutes.

Place the flour in a sieve. Shake about one-third of the flour over the egg mixture and gradually and very gently fold it in with a rubber spatula. Repeat adding the flour in two additions and folding it in until there are no streaks.

Spread the batter evenly in the prepared pans. Bake for 20 to 25 minutes, or until the tops are lightly browned and the cakes spring back when pressed lightly in the center. Cool for 10 minutes in the pans on wire racks.

Invert the cakes onto the racks and remove the pans. Carefully peel off the paper. Let cool completely upside down. (The layers can be made up to 2 days ahead. Wrap tightly in foil or plastic wrap.)

To assemble, place one cake layer on a serving plate. Spread the filling on top. Place the second cake layer on top.

For the decoration, knead the almond paste briefly to soften it. Place it in a food processor and add a drop of food coloring. Process until evenly tinted a light green, adding more color if needed. Turn the almond paste out onto a work surface. With your hands, shape it into a log. Wrap in plastic wrap until ready to use or use right away.

Cut the almond paste lengthwise into 4 slices. Place one slice between two sheets of wax paper. With a rolling pin, flatten it into a long narrow ribbon 2 inches wide and 1/8 inch thick. Trim off any rough edges. Repeat with the remaining almond paste. Wrap the almond paste around the sides of the cake, overlapping the ends slightly.

Gather any scraps of almond paste and reroll them. Cut the scraps into stars or hearts or ribbons with a fluted pasta cutter. Reserve for garnish.

To make the icing, whisk the egg whites, lemon zest, and juice in a medium bowl. Add the confectioners' sugar and stir until smooth.

Spread the icing evenly over the top of the cake. Decorate the cake with the almond paste shapes, if you made them, and the fruit. Refrigerate until serving time.

Sfogliatelle

Shfooyadell'

—◊◊◊—

Makes 12

For the Dough
3 cups unbleached all-purpose flour
1 teaspoon salt
1/4 cup solid vegetable shortening or lard
4 tablespoons unsalted butter
1 teaspoon honey
About 2/3 cup water

For the Filling
1 cup water
1/4 cup sugar
1/4 cup fine semolina or Cream of Wheat cereal
1 cup ricotta
1 large egg, beaten
1 teaspoon vanilla extract
1 teaspoon grated orange zest
1/4 teaspoon ground cinnamon
1/4 cup chopped candied citron or candied orange peel

To Assemble
1/2 cup solid vegetable shortening or lard
4 tablespoons unsalted butter
Confectioners' sugar

———— ✿ ✿ ✿ ————

To make the dough, put the flour and salt in a food processor, add the shortening and butter and pulse until the mixture resembles coarse crumbs. With the machine running, add the honey and about 1/2 cup of the water. Add more water a spoonful at a time as necessary until the dough begins to come together and form a ball. Transfer the dough to a lightly floured surface. Knead the dough for 1 minute, or until smooth. Flatten the dough into a disk and wrap it in plastic. Refrigerate for at least 1 hour, or overnight.

To make the filling, stir together the water, sugar, and semolina in a medium saucepan. Place over medium heat and bring to a simmer, stirring constantly. Cook for 2 minutes, or until the mixture is thick. Remove from the heat.

Stir in the ricotta, egg, vanilla, zest, and cinnamon. Mix in the candied citron. Cover and refrigerate until ready to use.

To shape the sfogliatelle, melt the shortening and butter in a small saucepan.

Divide the dough into 4 pieces. Place one piece on a lightly floured surface. Keep the remaining dough covered while you work. With a rolling pin, roll the dough out into a rectangle at least 24 inches long and 6 inches wide. Set the strip of dough aside while you roll out the remaining pieces in the same way.

Brush one strip of dough with the melted shortening and butter. Place a second strip on top and repeat the brushing. Stack and brush the remaining pieces in the same way.

Beginning at one of the narrow ends, tightly roll up the stack of dough into a log. Wrap in plastic wrap and refrigerate for at least one hour, or until firm. Cover the remaining shortening mixture and refrigerate.

Preheat the oven to 400°F. Line two large baking sheets with foil.

Trim the ends of the rolled-up dough to even them. Cut the dough into twelve 1/2-inch slices. Place one slice cut side down on a lightly floured surface. Center a rolling pin on the slice and roll first to the top, then to the bottom until the dough is thin. Place about 2 tablespoons of the filling to one side of the center. Fold the dough over and press the edges lightly to seal. Place the sfogliatelle on the prepared baking sheet. Continue making the remaining sfogliatelle in the same way.

Melt the reserved shortening mixture. Brush some over the pastries. Bake for 35 to 40 minutes, brushing two more times with the shortening, until the pastries are golden and crisp.

Slide the sfogliatelle onto a rack to cool slightly. Sprinkle with confectioners' sugar before serving.

Note: Sfogliatelle are best served warm. If making them ahead, let them cool completely, then refrigerate or freeze them tightly wrapped in plastic. Reheat in a 350°F oven for 10 minutes.

Afterword

BY ARTIE BUCCO

Well, there you have it. *La cucina nostra.* Our food. I hope you take these recipes to hearth and home and have a thousand meals and a thousand laughs. As Charmaine so beautifully put it, food is the glue of tradition, blood ties, and good health. Being so, it should never be dismissed as merely "something to eat."

Given that you've read this far in the book, I'm probably preaching to the choir here, but I must end with one final plea. Please, don't move through this hurly-burly modern world so fast that you forget to stop and enjoy the celebration of eating. Do you want your kids growing up and passing on to *their* kids your junk food love of ranch-style chips or the double-bacon cheeseburger? How sad is that? No matter who you are, you come from somewhere, and that somewhere has a tradition of native foodstuffs that in part define you. If, for any reason, you can't locate that tradition, then join us at the Italian-American table and eat our food. You could do worse.

Buon appetito!

the end

Index of Recipes

Allen Rucker is the author of the best-selling *The Sopranos: A Family History*, as well as two books of satire with Martin Mull, *The History of White People In America* and *A Paler Shade of White*. He's also an award-winning TV writer/producer and lives in Los Angeles.

Michele Scicolone is the author of several Italian cookbooks and teaches cooking classes around the country. Her most recent book is *Italian Holiday Cooking* published by William Morrow. She writes frequently for the *Washington Post* and major food and wine magazines. She grew up in Bensonhurst, Brooklyn, and all of her grandparents come from the Naples area, not far from the Soprano family.